Life at 36,000 Feet

Where Faith and Fear Connect

by
Sharon Carroll Williams

LIFE AT 36,000 FEET: Where Faith and Fear Connect
by Sharon Carroll Williams

© 2021 Sharon Carroll Williams

Published by SCW62 Books

ISBN 978-1-7368938-0-7

Original Cover Art by Rick Kersten: kerstengallery.com

Graphic Design Cover Work by Next Generation Designs

Dedication

For my husband Dale, for his love, his support of my career, and his encouragement for me to write.

For my parents, who taught me about God's love and instilled in me a love of travel.

For my daughter, Amanda, a beautiful young woman who will now understand the job that took her mom away at times.

For my grandson, Tanner, who gives me so much joy and laughter.

And last but not least, for Bob Poole, who gave me my first chance to enter the world of aviation.

Life at 36,000 Feet

Where Faith and Fear Connect

Table of Contents

PART IV: AMERICAN AIRLINES

Foreword

No other career holds a candle to that of a flight attendant. I served as one for thirty-four years, so I've pretty much seen it all by this point. From lost dentures to lost children, from frightened parrots to phobic passengers, my cabins have experienced a whirlwind of activity.

Life in the sky also brings camaraderie and intrigue. Every day differs because we get to observe so many people going in different directions. Sometimes the crew members know each other well, so it's like flying with friends, and other times, crews who have never met fly together, which means a chance for new connections.

Communication between the captain and flight attendants is always crucial because life in the air is unlike that on the ground. For instance, if a passenger is rude or unruly, flight attendants can't simply leave the aircraft to get away from them. We can't call 911 or law enforcement to help us, and although we can choose to go to the other end of the airplane, the passenger can always find us!

More than anything, we depend on our imaginations to get us through each flight. If the catering department fails to supply the correct number of entrees, we improvise because we don't have the convenience of a nearby grocery store or a freezer full of extra casseroles. But through all the minor and major emergencies, we put on smiling faces so that passengers don't suspect a thing. Every flight, we roll with the punches—and the turbulence—to give passengers the smoothest experience possible.

My Solution to the Fear Factor

For many, the fear of flying is very real. Some of my dearest friends and family do not fly because of what they refer to as the "fear factor." Over the years, many aerophobes have confided that their anxiety stems from an inability to control their own destiny while in the air. With some of them, I share my personal philosophy: It is unlikely that any of us are in control of our own fate. I tell them that I believe one's fate is in God's hands. Of course, that's a hard message for some to accept; it doesn't resonate with everyone.

Back in 1990, I flew with a new flight attendant who confessed that she didn't like to fly. I found that unusual until I learned that she had only entered the field of aviation because her dad was a pilot and she thought he would approve of her career path. When we took off on our first flight together, she closed her eyes and grabbed my arm. Not a good start to her career. When we encountered an emergency later in the trip, it became obvious that she would have to find her own personal philosophy if she were to make it in the industry.

I experienced three onboard emergency situations during my years as a flight attendant, but God protected me during those incidents. I continued flying without fear because I had faith that He ultimately controlled my fate, regardless of whether my feet were on the ground or thousands of feet above it.

Adventure

My job offered pure adventure. During my career, I visited all fifty US states, twelve different countries, and fourteen islands, as part of work or on personal vacations. As my years of service built up, the trips drastically improved. This book shares the true stories I collected over my thirty-four-year career as a flight attendant. Each trip became its own adventure, some of which were experienced on the aircraft itself

Welcome to my *Life at 36,000 Feet*!

Part I

Piedmont Airlines

"The will of God will never take us
where the grace of God will not sustain us."

~ Billy Graham

Chapter 1

BREAK

Late on a dreary February morning in 2018, I rushed around my bedroom and packed my suitcase for a three-day trip to San Francisco, leaving at 6:00 p.m. out of Charlotte, North Carolina. Charlotte served as my flight attendant base, so all of my flights started and ended there. Airline crews were allowed to live anywhere in the world they chose, but they had to be dependable and rely on their flying privileges of "space available priority" to get to their bases when needed. Given that I lived in Roanoke, a small community in the Blue Ridge Mountains of southwest Virginia, my first necessity whenever I booked a trip was to make sure I could get a flight to Charlotte. If I couldn't, it meant a four-hour drive, something I did about 25 percent of the time.

After packing—a task I could do on autopilot after thirty-four years in the industry—I checked my watch. I had just enough time to do a favor for my friend Trena. She wanted my opinion on a terrier she was considering adopting from my neighbor Cecile, a dog lover and rescuer. I told my husband, Dale, that I would be back in a minute.

Since it was raining, I drove to Cecile's house a couple doors down. As I hurried up the sidewalk to her porch, I could hear the barks of her multiple dogs. After I rang the bell, Cecile motioned for me to come inside, but as I pushed the door open, the puppy rushed past me and escaped.

I ran after him, chasing him across the street and then back across to another neighbor's yard. When he dashed up a grassy, muddy hill, I didn't waver in my pursuit. But about four strides up the incline, I slipped and fell awkwardly, thudding to the ground as an audible break reached my ears.

The pain in my leg was excruciating, like nothing I'd ever felt before. I screamed for help, though I feared the pounding rain might drown out my cries. As I waited for Cecile to find me, things only got worse. I made the mistake of looking down, and what I saw could in no way be construed as positive. My left foot was pointing in the opposite direction than it usually pointed.

Foolishly, I tried to get up, but that was a losing proposition. Thankfully, Cecile appeared beside me moments later.

"I think I broke my hip," I cried.

Cecile, a spiritual person who always called on God first, took a moment to lean in and say a prayer over me. Then she pulled out her phone and called 911 as I lay on the cold ground in the pouring rain. Luckily, her husband had followed her out and brought a blanket to cover me—just in time, too, because I could tell I was going into shock.

Two male EMTs arrived within five minutes. The taller one took one look at my twisted leg, shook his head, and said, "I'm afraid you've got a broken femur."

7

"But isn't that the largest bone in my body?" I asked.

"It sure is. We're going to have to put your left leg in a splint in order to transport you." Before they did, they gave me something for the unbelievable pain, but I still yelped as they lifted me into the emergency vehicle.

Needless to say, I wouldn't be heading to Charlotte that day. When the EMTs gave me yet another shot for the unbearable stabs of agony emanating from my leg, I closed my eyes and reflected on my career in the sky. I retraced memories of how it all began and wondered if I would ever be able to endure the long hours on my feet again, traipsing up and down the aisle, tending to passengers' needs and loving every minute of it.

Chapter 2

AVIATION

At age twenty-six, I entered the world of aviation. I had signed up for a night class at a local college in 1981 and found myself sitting behind another student named Cindy Gibson. She and I chatted between lectures and became instant friends. To this day, I believe our meeting was providential because she helped me change my life.

Cindy worked for the City of Roanoke, while I worked at a local savings and loan. When I mentioned that I was unhappy with my job, she told me of an open secretarial position for the Roanoke Municipal Airport manager. I don't believe in luck; I believe that God puts you in the places He wants you to be at the moments in time that may change your life. This was one of those moments.

I felt excited at the prospect of changing careers and possibly traveling, especially since I had only flown twice in my life. When I was growing up, my family explored forty of the fifty US states by car. We'd venture out every summer on different vacations. On most of those trips, we'd camp out, and I have fond memories of relaxing by the fire, playing board games with my brother and sister after supper, and sharing valuable time with my family, but I came to believe that only rich people could afford to *fly* somewhere on vacation.

I eagerly filled out the job application and was called for an interview the same week. As I entered the airport terminal, I noticed all of the busy people, rushing with their suitcases for the gates, and the lines of people standing patiently at each ticket counter. I could not help but wonder what all their destinations were.

When I stepped inside the airport manager's office, I saw the friendly face of an old high school classmate. He told me he had already put in a good word for me with his boss. I smiled and thanked him, confiding that I needed all the help I could get. To my dismay, the manager, a man named Bob Poole, was already interviewing another job candidate in his office, most likely my competition. My foot tapped against the floor like a snare drummer's stick, but I tried to hide my nervousness when the office door opened. After Mr. Poole strode toward me with a smile, I shook his hand and introduced myself.

We got along immediately. His encouraging words and hearty laugh reassured me, and although I had never before worked as a secretary, I had the necessary skills such as shorthand and typing that were required for the job. Mr. Poole mentioned that I had provided two good references but was lacking some necessary experience. I told him I was currently taking classes to improve my skills and felt that I could fill the position if he would only give me the chance. He said he would make a final decision by end of the following week.

Upon leaving, I felt very discouraged, but the following week, he called and told me I got the job. I began my new career two weeks later, and I have been thankful ever since that I had the opportunity to work for him. It gave me valuable opportunities to learn about the field of aviation and how an airport operates on a day-to-day basis.

One day, Bob asked me to take dictation for several letters he wanted to send out. Outfitted in a cute pink sundress, I went into his office with my pen and tablet in hand, ready to fulfill the requested task. After successfully taking the dictation, I stood up to leave but suddenly felt a cold draft on my back.

"I think you're losing something," Bob exclaimed.

I reached back to find that my zipper had broken and my sundress was open to my hips! I must admit that was one of the most embarrassing moments in my life, but Bob handled it like a gentleman. He quickly removed his jacket, put it on my shoulders, and suggested the name of a woman in the office who might be able to help fix the zipper. After many valiant attempts and much frustration, she couldn't fix it, so I resorted to going home and changing. That memory sticks with me as if it happened yesterday.

One of my regular duties was to collect rent from the tenants on the airport property. I used my car the first couple of months, but someone suggested that I get a motorcycle license, which would allow me to drive a three-wheel vehicle owned by the City of Roanoke. I did, thereby making for a little more adventure whenever I put on my motorcycle helmet and drove the superspeed vehicle— nicknamed "Buzzard One"—from hangar to hangar. A news reporter saw me making my rounds one day, so he took a picture of ole Buzz and me, and we were featured in an article in the Roanoke Times that week. It was quite the talk around the airport for a while.

As I collected rents, I enjoyed hearing the various stories of the local pilots. It became clear that, to them, a career in aviation was more than a job; it was a lifestyle. I would hear expressions like, "You just wait—aviation and flying will get in your blood." I guess that eventually happened without me even realizing it.

Another responsibility was to greet each person that entered our office, and I often filled them in on fees, rules, and regulations pertaining to airport operations. As it turned out, I enjoyed the public relations aspect of the job much more than dictation and typing, which told me deep down that God must have had something else in store for my future. I longed for a job that had more freedom and more contact with people, so I made it my goal to find such an opportunity—until one special day when I realized I was expecting my first child. I excitedly told Bob the news. He was a father of four himself, so he shared my excitement.

Later that day, a bouquet of flowers arrived with a card that read, "For my first secretary with one in the hangar." It meant so much that he shared my joy. I continued working despite horrible morning sickness, and my daughter, Amanda, was born in June 1982. She was and still is truly one of my biggest blessings, but as many people know, new realties and conflicts develop once you become a mother with a full-time job. Your heart and priorities sometimes pull you in different directions, and mine certainly did. I had longed for a child for several years, and it pained me to leave her every day.

Once I returned from maternity leave, I still loved my job, but I felt a restlessness. Part of me wanted to stay home more, so I decided to find a part-time job as soon as possible. A few days later, as I ate lunch in the airport restaurant, a friend shared with me that the Piedmont Airlines flight attendant manager needed a part-time secretary. I discussed this potential change of career with my husband, and we figured we could make it work. The next day, I headed to the flight attendant office. It was upstairs from where I already worked, so I vaguely knew Al Kirk, the manager. He was known to be a nice man who was wonderful to work for. We discussed the possibility of my becoming a Piedmont Airlines employee, and after some discussion, he offered me the position.

Giving notice at a job I enjoyed was not easy, but I had a good reason. I explained to Bob my desire to work part-time and be home more with my daughter. He fully understood, and we left on good terms.

I will forever be thankful for the opportunity that was given to me. I look back now and wonder how I ever landed that first job that introduced me to the world of aviation. Only God could have helped direct Bob to take a chance on me as his secretary when there were many others more qualified.

While in the flight attendant office, my world became the world of airports, airlines, and travel. I learned aviation tips that proved beneficial for my future, and I learned firsthand what it was like for the flight attendants to travel and have flexible schedules. After working in the office for a year, I approached Al about the possibility of becoming a flight attendant. He reluctantly told me that while I would make a good flight attendant, he had just gotten me trained and would have to replace me. But a tug at my heart told me that flight attendant was the job God wanted me to do. After Al's recommendation and well wishes, I interviewed for the position, and after a slew of interviews and written tests, I was selected to start a training class on July 2, 1984. Approximately four thousand applicants a month applied for the position of a flight attendant, so I felt lucky to have been chosen.

The training would be in Winston-Salem, North Carolina and would last four weeks. I was relieved to know that I could go home on weekends and see my family. Though I dreaded being away for so long, I knew I had to do it in order to start my new career.

One major advantage of the job was that Piedmont paid full benefits and the opportunity for flight attendants to drop trips if they did not want to fly weekly, which meant I could have more time at home and the chance to earn a better income.

A job and lifestyle involving travel had never been a goal of mine in my youth, but God had other plans. He places ideas, people, and situations in our paths for a reason, His reason. And so began my career in the sky, but first I had to get the necessary training I would need to succeed.

Chapter 3

TRAINING

On July 2, 1984, I arrived in Winston-Salem, nervous but excited. My first stop was to check in at the nearby hotel. As I stood in line and chatted with the people behind me, I met Mary, a fellow trainee from Wilmington, North Carolina. We discussed what we had heard about the training and shared some of the same concerns. When the hotel clerk asked me if I had requested a roommate, I turned to my new friend and, without putting a lot of thought behind it, explained, "I'm here to study and not here to party. If you feel the same way, maybe we can room together." She readily agreed that she was there to study too, and so began our long friendship. From then on, we helped each other study the aircraft schematics, learn the evacuation commands, and prepare for the daily quizzes. We still laugh today about my abrupt remark.

In the first week of training, we were expected to undergo weight checks and eye exams. Both had restrictions attached, and if we did not pass, we wouldn't progress in the program. We also underwent a hair and makeup evaluation. My "Farrah Fawcett" hairstyle was quite popular at the time, but our superiors did not like it, so my hair was cut into a more professional style during the second week. I also learned which colors looked best on me, as determined by skin tone and hair color. I admit that I looked different after my makeover, with shorter, darker hair and makeup shades from the "autumn" section of the color palette. They wanted us to look our best—or at least their version of our best.

We spent the last couple weeks of training learning the serving techniques, and then the big day arrived. We actually got to train on flights in and out of Greensboro, North Carolina. This was the closest airport to our training center. The first time that I stepped onboard the Boeing 737 as a new trainee, I was so afraid I was going to spill coffee on a passenger, forget the sequence of the service procedure, or make a mistake during the announcements. But despite being a bundle of nerves, I managed to finally feel comfortable. As we trainees entered and announced that we were handling the onboard service, the actual flight attendants smiled, knowing they could relax and not work the flight. I later enjoyed having new hires on my flights, and I always reassured them that I survived my training flights and overcame the accompanying anxieties.

As I progressed in my career, people often asked, "What could be so hard about learning how to give out peanuts and drinks?" But there was more to it than that. The training was rigorous and stressful. We had to learn not only the details of each aircraft but emergency drills, CPR, and other medical procedures. Each trainee had to be proficient in all areas and score 90 percent or above on most quizzes to continue with the instruction. Though we never knew for certain whose grades fell below the required minimum, some classmates did mysteriously disappear, never to be seen again. Also, we were under constant observation because the instructors needed to ensure that we were dependable, flexible, and able to best represent the airline.

Four weeks later, our wings were pinned to our uniforms, and we received a certificate. We all breathed a sigh of relief. As new flight attendants for Piedmont Airlines, we were allowed to request the flight attendant base we desired. I, of course, chose Roanoke, Virginia. Little did I know then some of the challenges that lay in store for me.

Chapter 4

HOOK

One of my first flights with Piedmont was from Roanoke, Virginia, to LaGuardia, New York, on a Boeing 727, the largest jet we flew at the time. As I picked up the trays after the meal and beverage service, the male passenger in seat 8D asked me to help him to the bathroom. I told him to follow me to the back of the aircraft, where I pointed to the restroom. He stepped inside but then turned and asked me if I could assist him.

Taken aback, I maintained a straight face and asked, "You need my help in the bathroom?"

In response, he dropped the jacket he was holding to reveal two hooks in place of his hands. "I can't unzip my pants."

I glanced between the hooks and his pleading eyes several times. "Are you flying with someone who can help you?"

"No, I'm alone, and I can't wait much longer."

He sounded frustrated, and I could sympathize, even though I'd certainly never been in a similar situation. But still, I didn't feel comfortable stepping into the small, enclosed space with him to do such a personal favor. I told him I'd be back in a moment and went in search of my coworker.

"That's a new one for me," she said after I explained.

I returned to the anxious, uncomfortable man and told him with regret that while I could not enter the bathroom with him, I would try to find someone else to assist him.

"What am I supposed to do in the meantime?" he asked. We stared at each other. I knew that as a flight attendant, I was supposed to be able to provide an answer to every possible onboard situation, but this one had me flustered.

"Go back to your seat while I find someone." He picked up his jacket, draped it over his hooks, and reluctantly returned to his seat.

I had no idea what to do, so I called the cockpit and explained the situation to the First Officer.

"You want me to do *what*?" he said.

I laughed nervously, even though it wasn't a laughing matter, and told him I wasn't kidding. "The man seems desperate for help."

"Okay, but it's going to be a few minutes until I can leave the cockpit."

Fifteen minutes passed before he emerged from the cockpit, and I apologized again for having to make such an awkward request. We approached the poor man in seat 8D, and I tapped him on the shoulder.

"One of our pilots is here to help you, sir," I said quietly so as not to attract too much attention.

In response, he pointed to his wet seat cushion. "I don't need your help anymore. I took care of it." I asked him if he would like to move to a dry seat, and he agreed that would be a good idea. Once we landed, the seat cushion was removed and replaced.

I felt terrible for that passenger, but I also felt I had done everything I could have to help under the circumstances. After I joined my coworkers in the rear of the plane, they asked what had happened. They agreed I had done the only thing possible and that the only alternative would have been to ask a male passenger to help, but that too would have been a very awkward request.

Flight attendants never know what unusual situations they will be called upon to resolve. There are no training manuals that outline awkward situations, so we must often use our imaginations to solve the new problems that arise every day. Our objective is to make the travel experience as comfortable and stress-free as possible, but in that particular instance, the outcome of my plan was not what I had anticipated.

Empathy, a word that was stressed over and over in our flight attendant training, means the ability to understand and share the feelings of another. That situation with the desperate passenger required it, and I tried to employ it. Sometimes we succeed, but sometimes we do not. During most interactions with passengers, I tried to put myself in "their seat" and feel their pain. I think it helped me to be a better flight attendant, who strove to do her best in every situation.

I later wrote a note to my supervisor explaining what had happened that day. I asked her if there were any onboard rules that would have helped. She replied that I had done all I could do at the time and admitted it was an unusual situation that was likely to only happen once in a career.

We never know when we will encounter unusual situations—on or off an aircraft. The Bible clearly teaches us to help others in need in Matthew 7:12, a scripture known as the Golden Rule: "Do unto others as you would have them do unto you." In other words, treat others how you want to be treated. This rule was taught to me as a child growing up in a Christian home. It's an important rule to live by, and one of my most fervent wishes is that we would all practice it daily, especially in a world where discord and divisiveness sometimes rule the day. With God's help, it makes it a lot easier to say yes when those around us ask for assistance.

Chapter 5

DRUNK

As the months flew by—literally—I enjoyed my career in the sky. One of the main reasons was that I experienced places and activities that, until then, I had only read about. My first year of flying included layovers in cities I'd never visited, so I spent those valuable hours sightseeing and taking tours. When I had a twenty-three-hour break in New York City, I took the opportunity to see my first Broadway play. What a dream to be working and spending time that felt like a paid vacation.

Other crew members would say they could always spot new flight attendants because during layovers, the newbies would change clothes and be on the streets of the city in a matter of minutes. That was me! I got into the habit of signing up for bus tours as soon as I got to a city that I wanted to visit, and I kept a journal so I could spend more time at my favorite places during the next layover.

Piedmont was unique because it served small airports that no other airlines serviced. One such location was Jacksonville, North Carolina, which people routinely confused with Jacksonville, Florida. More than once after making the onboard announcement that we were traveling to North Carolina, not Florida, several call bells would ring because ticketholders realized they were on the wrong flight.

One day, we were boarding a flight from Charlotte to Jacksonville, North Carolina. I was the lead "A" flight attendant, which meant I would report any problems in the cabin directly to the captain. The captain and I would then consult and decide how to address the problem. This short flight was full of soldiers from the military base in Jacksonville, and I noticed one soldier assisting the other as they entered through the forward door. I greeted them with a smile but observed that one of them did not make eye contact with me.

We were halfway through the process of boarding when several call bells rang in the back section. Catherine, the "B" flight attendant, quickly assessed the problem and called me on the intercom.

"One of the soldiers is drunk!" she exclaimed. "He's slumped over the lady in the window seat, and we can't wake him up. Not only that but he threw up on her and she is furious!"

I stopped the boarding and asked the passengers to remain at the door for a few minutes while I made my way down the narrow aisle to row 12. The drunk man's buddy, the one I had noticed earlier, looked up and said, "I think we have a problem."

I nodded in agreement, leaned over, and tried to wake up the inebriated soldier. This went on for several minutes. The soldier's friend shook him, yelled at him, and punched him, but nothing worked. He was out cold.

"Soldier or not," I said, "we cannot transport a passenger who is drunk." The putrid smell filled the hot, cramped cabin. Passengers began to complain about the odor, while others questioned why we hadn't finished boarding yet. I requested that the trapped woman try crawling over the unconscious soldier, but she refused and declared that she had an important meeting in Jacksonville. I ended up handing her some club soda and a towel because that is a flight attendant's go-to remedy for removing all stains. Apparently, this gave the soldier's friend an idea. He stood up and threw cold water in the man's face. Still nothing.

"Can't we just let him sleep it off?" the friend asked.

By now I was fighting back waves of nausea. "No, we can't take him. He needs to get off the plane."

I walked to the cockpit and asked the Captain for permission to remove the drunk passenger. He said he would call security to remove him. In the meantime, the two other flight attendants tried to restore order in the cabin.

"We will now continue our boarding and will be leaving shortly," I announced to the seated passengers. Security arrived, and I directed them to the sleeping soldier. They had to use a wheelchair to get him off the plane, and as they passed me, they remarked that they couldn't rouse him either. The guy was completely out!

I sometimes wonder what that soldier thought when he woke up and found himself sitting in an office in Charlotte, North Carolina, but one thing is for sure: I imagine he thinks twice now before indulging in too many preflight cocktails.

In my life, I noticed that each new experience on the

aircraft seemed to offer a new lesson that I could apply to my own life, even if it was learned via the mistakes of others. I believe we all can find things out the hard way and suffer the consequences, but we can also learn from others and avoid suffering their misfortunes. From this incident, I learned that moderation is best, just like with most things in life. After all, my choice between moderation and overindulgence might one day determine if I find myself waking up in the wrong airport.

Chapter 6

BABYSITTER

Some of my favorite trips were to the west coast. I love California and its beautiful scenery. Whenever I had a twenty-four-hour layover there, I made it a point to explore something new and different. I generally worked the red-eye flights so I could enjoy a full day of sightseeing. "Red-eye" is the term the airlines use to describe a flight that leaves late in the evening and flies all night, arriving at the destination the following morning. It refers to the sleepy red eyes we have when we land.

San Francisco quickly became one of my favorite cities, and as Union Square was near our hotel, I always took a brisk morning walk there once I had a few hours of sleep. Twice I met celebrities on the street. One time in Union Square, I was standing on a corner waiting for the light to turn when I heard two nearby women squealing with delight. When I looked to my left, there stood Beyoncé!

"Are you performing here tonight?" I asked.

She laughed and said she could not believe I knew who she was. I told her how much I loved her music, and we parted ways when the light changed. It was only a short encounter, but she struck me as a nice lady. She had probably wondered how I recognized her because she was wearing no makeup and had a baseball cap on her head, but she simply stood out. That was my usual attire too as I busily hurried around looking for local art, stopping at street vendors who sold handmade pieces of jewelry, and occasionally shopping in one of the big department stores.

On one beautiful morning there, I sipped my coffee and admired the Bay City through my hotel window. I called another coworker and asked if she wanted to go to Polk Street for breakfast. She agreed, and we had a fantastic meal. Afterward, we decided to do what a lot of flight attendants do on layovers: get a manicure. As we crossed California Street, I ran smack into a man walking in the opposite direction. When I looked up to apologize, I could barely get any words out because I was staring at the face of Nicolas Cage. "I'm sorry," I said, "but aren't you Nicolas Cage?"

"I sure am!" he said, then we both hurried out of the middle of the street because a cable car was fast approaching.

Haley

During one layover, my friend Trena and I rented bikes and rode across the Golden Gate Bridge. It was so exhilarating to see the beautiful bay and city from that perspective. We continued across the bridge to Sausalito and enjoyed lunch at an outdoor café while we watched the boats sail back and forth on the glistening water. Of course, it wasn't nearly as easy to pedal back to where we had started, given our full stomachs.

When we finally reached the hotel, we rested for six hours before heading to the airport for a five-hour flight to Charlotte. I was the "B" flight attendant, and as I boarded and checked the passengers, I noticed a young mother and her daughter, who looked to be four or five years old. The mother put several bags in the overhead bin. After they were seated in 18A and 18B, the mother rang the call bell and requested a blanket and a pillow. We always kept both onboard to make the passengers more comfortable, so I handed her the items. Then she asked if we had any eye masks for sleeping. I told her that we didn't but that the lights would be turned off after we finished our beverage service.

Red-eye flights are not for everyone, and some flight attendants don't enjoy them. The lights are turned off after the last service round, and the flight attendants generally spend time in the front or back galleys, trying to stay awake. To keep from falling asleep, I usually read a book or walked through the cabin, checking the passengers to make sure they were okay. On one of those walkabouts, as I made my way through the darkness, I accidentally stepped on a man's foot that was projected into the aisle. I must have scared him out of a deep sleep because he kicked me. He apologized afterward and confided that he was a veteran who sometimes hit people while dreaming. Upon returning to the back galley, I told the other attendants what had happened, and they looked to see if I had any bruises on my leg. That led to a conversation about the noises and smells that can accompany a red-eye flight, and we agreed that some of them were pretty disgusting. About that time, a small voice sounded out behind me.

"Where is my mommy?"

I turned to see the cute little girl from 18B, who looked like she was about to cry. I took her hand and told her I would find her mother, which I did. She was curled in her seat, covered with a blanket and sleeping against the window. I leaned over and tapped her on the shoulder, waking her. She stared up at me in a sleepy daze.

"I'm returning your daughter to you. She was walking around lost in the cabin." I spoke softly so as to not wake up the other passengers. The mother scolded her daughter, Haley, to stay seated, and before I even walked away, she had covered herself with the blanket and turned back toward the window to sleep. I laughed to myself and then shared the story with my fellow crew members.

"I hope she stays in her seat this time," I said. "Maybe she'll fall asleep too."

We were two hours from Charlotte, and the flight had been a quiet one so far. Just as I asked the other two flight attendants if they wanted me to make coffee or hot tea to help us stay awake, the call bell went off in the cabin. As I went to answer it, I was met by four people hovering around row 10. There was Haley, standing in their midst.

"She was running up and down the aisle waking us all up," said one rotund man. "We've been trying to find her mother."

"Haley, take my hand," I said, "and I'll take you to your mommy." We headed back to row 18 and I once again woke the mother, telling her as politely as I could to please keep her daughter in her seat. "It's important," I informed her, "because we're expected to get light turbulence soon."

As I walked off, she yelled from her seat, "Isn't this part of your job?" I turned around to face her. "Isn't it part of your job to watch our kids while we sleep?"

I couldn't believe what I was hearing. I walked over to her and without hesitation said, "It is your responsibility as her mother to watch her." As exhausted as I was, I tried to keep my voice calm.

"I'm really tired," she whined, "and I know you all aren't doing anything now."

"I'm sorry, but that's not an option." I couldn't see her face clearly in the darkness, but I imagine she wasn't very happy with my answer. It was one of the first times I realized that some passengers don't know or care about what our job is.

Whenever I think about little Haley wandering around in the dark, waking up passengers and trying to find her mommy, it reminds me of mankind trying to find happiness. We all are looking for fulfillment and purpose in life. Sometimes it takes someone to help lead the way. In my life, it was Jesus Christ who stepped into my life when I was only nine years old and helped me find direction and purpose. He has been my constant and best friend who has helped me in difficult situations. I wish I could say I haven't gotten lost along the way, but one thing I know is that He didn't move; rather, I did. He always welcomes us back with open arms, forgives us, and grants us another chance even when we don't deserve one. Like a child wandering around on a dark aircraft, many of us are looking for happiness and purpose in this dark world. It is the light of God that will truly show us the way.

Chapter 7

FEAR

As mentioned earlier, the fear of flying is very real for some people. I had many conversations with those who suffer from phobias, and the fears of snakes, spiders, heights, and especially flying are high on the list. Frightened passengers have admitted that they feel they cannot control their destiny when they are in the air because the plane is under the control of others. Some people have flown in such turbulent weather that they never want to fly again.

My dad was with me years ago on a small propeller (prop) plane going from Roanoke to New York. Twenty minutes into the flight, the air got so turbulent that even I had white knuckles. To this day, though my father can fly for free as part of my benefits package, he would rather drive than fly. He still talks about and relives that one horrible flight.

Several years ago, I was working a full flight on a large 737-400 to Los Angles. Piedmont had added the bigger jets to the fleet when it expanded westward. The plane had only one aisle, but it was nevertheless capable of making longer flights. Though the passengers must have been uncomfortable, squeezed together for five to six hours, most of them endured it without complaint.

The boarding was nothing out of the ordinary except for the fact that a middle-aged man asked to meet our captain before we even left the gate. We accommodated him, and the two men shook hands. Immediately, the passenger peppered the captain with questions.

How long have you been flying? How old is this aircraft? The captain cordially answered all the queries and seemed to satisfy the passenger, who then headed to his seat in 17F. As was customary, we made the preliminary announcement that we would be flying to Los Angeles with an approximate flying time of six hours. As we made our ascent out of Philadelphia, a call bell went off in the cabin, but flight attendants are required to remain in their jump seats during takeoff, so I made an announcement. "We are required to remain seated during takeoff. If this is a true emergency, please ring your call bell again."

The bell went off a second time. It was the man who had spoken to the captain. A few minutes later, when it was safe to walk to his seat, I did so. "What can I help you with, sir?"

"I'm nervous and hate to fly," he said. "Can I have a double Jack and Coke?"

I told him he would have to wait a short while until the aircraft leveled off, and then we would begin our beverage service. But I could tell he was not accustomed to waiting. Twenty minutes later, the call bell sounded again, and I realized it was our impatient friend again in 17F. I left the beverage cart and approached his seat, but I already knew what he wanted.

"I've waited long enough," he said. "You know what I need."

I was losing patience with him, but I said in a calm voice that I would get his drink for him.

"I mean, I'll just be a lot happier if I can get some whiskey in me."

I hoped it was true as I brought him his cocktail.

As we were finishing the beverage and meal service, the call bell went off again.

"Oh no!" I exclaimed to my coworker. "It's 17F again. Would you take care of him this time?"

She agreed. Predictably, when she got to his seat, he asked for another Jack and Coke and requested that she bring drinks for his many new friends who were seated around him. She returned to the cart and prepared six cocktails.

"Maybe this double will be enough to make him sleepy," she said with a laugh.

With four hours left in the flight, we hoped he wouldn't ring his bell every fifteen minutes. Walking through the cabin later, I noticed that he had indeed fallen asleep under the spell of the liquor. But he was snoring loudly—so loudly, in fact, that people around him were starting to complain. Thank goodness it was time for the onboard movie to begin. We decided to handle the snoring issue by giving the passengers around him complimentary headphones. Often, when nothing else worked, free items helped soothe away problems.

After a while, we heard a loud banging noise in the cabin, and multiple call bells rang out. I immediately ran up the aisle to row 17. As several passengers screamed, the disruptive man in 17F banged his head against the wall beside his seat. I asked him to stop, but he fixed his eyes on me and said he couldn't control himself, that his fears had taken over his rationality. He demanded to be let off the plane.

I asked the passengers seated in his row to please let him get out of his window seat. I'd learned over the years that a sense of confinement sometimes bothers passengers. They let him out, and he managed to follow me to the back galley, where I gave him my "nervous passenger" speech. I reminded him that statistically he was much safer in the air than on a busy highway, but after ten minutes of reassurance, he didn't seem any calmer. Under my breath, I asked the other two flight attendants to stand in front of the back doors because I didn't know what he might do next.

"What is it about flying that really scares you?" I asked him.

"Not being in charge of my own life. And you know what else?" He pointed to a random woman in the cabin. "What if it's *her* time to go? Wouldn't that mean I'm going with her?"

I looked at him in dismay. He really felt that way, and his fears were consuming him. There was nothing I could say to calm the poor man's hysteria, but I could control my next request of him. I asked him to remain with us in the back galley to talk for a while. We asked him about his family, his job, and what his plans were when he got to Los Angeles. Once he began talking, he seemed to relax and forget he was in the air. He even told a few jokes and never mentioned his fears again. When it was time to take his seat again, he smiled and apologized that he had acted so silly.

I hope that his flight back to the east coast was easier, and I hope that he learned to deter his fears by talking.

Have you ever had a major fear of something in your life? I have. I used to be afraid of speaking in public. I would tremble and sweat, and my heart would feel like it was beating out of my chest when I had to speak. The medical term for such a fear is glossophobia, and it affects as many as four out of ten Americans. As a child, whenever my church youth group led special services, I would stutter and feel sick to my stomach while speaking in front of the congregation. Despite my phobia, I ran for class offices in high school, but I still got hives before delivering a speech. Precisely because of my fear, I decided to push myself to speak in public. When I worked for a Savings and Loan Association in my twenties, I competed in the National Speech Contest for several years. For some reason, I felt compelled to overcome my fear, and I finally did. Little did I know when I was a trembling young mess breaking out in hives that I would eventually speak to the public on a regular basis, making aircraft announcements many times a day.

I challenge each of you to take control of your fears. Don't let them isolate you and make you feel helpless. Do what you can to overcome them and change your life for the better.

When you feel like the battle is hopeless, perhaps you'll think of this scripture from Philippians 4:13: "I can do all things through Christ who strengthens me."

Chapter 8

EMERGENCY

In late 1986, we heard rumors that the airline might be sold or merged with another airline. In February of 1987, Piedmont Aviation, Inc., the parent company of Piedmont Airlines, received takeover offers from several companies, and the Board of Directors recommended approval of the bid by the Norfolk Southern Railroad Corporation, mainly because Norfolk Southern already owned 19.4 percent of Piedmont stock. The successful railroad company was based in Roanoke, Virginia, where I lived at the time. The news shocked many of the employees, but after much deliberation, Piedmont and Norfolk Southern failed to come to an agreement, which opened the way for another interested company to make a bid. That company was USAir, and all conversation between crew members turned to what our future might be.

In the Roanoke crew room, I chatted with fellow employees about possible mergers and what they might mean. We all knew one thing for sure: a merger meant major changes, maybe even layoffs and base closings. As a single mom, I was particularly concerned about Piedmont's fate.

That day, I left for a three-day trip on the 737-200 aircraft, which required three flight attendants. We had a good crew, and we enjoyed some nice layovers in Nashville, Tennessee, and Baltimore, Maryland. On the last leg of our trip back to Roanoke, we were busy preparing the cabin for landing and feeling relieved to have finished our trip. As we discussed what we would do on our upcoming days off, I shared my philosophy: the first day after a trip, you catch up on rest, and the next day, you run errands to catch up on life. We could choose to fly one- to four-day trips, and my usual choice was a two- or three-day trip because I didn't want to be away from my daughter, Amanda, for long. I loved my job, but on the downside, it took me away from her. Though her dad and grandmother kept her while I was away, I sometimes felt a sense of guilt at the separation. I had divorced in early 1986, which had made life a bit more complicated.

If you have ever been a single parent, you know that juggling a career and raising a child doesn't make for the easiest life. As best I could, I strove to fly the required hours and be home for my daughter's many activities. No one ever intends to divorce when they marry the person they love, but sometimes life changes and leaves you in a challenging situation. Adjustments need to be made, and more help is required from family and friends. Thank goodness I had help from so many along the way during those early years, though it was still hard for Amanda to have her mom away from home a couple nights a week. Every job has its ups and downs, and that was surely one of the downs for us.

Meanwhile, back to our flight…

As we chatted, a bell rang to signal that the pilots were readying to make the final approach for landing. All proceeded normally except for a signal that followed, which was a call from the cockpit. The lead flight attendant, Kelly, held a brief conversation with the pilot, then turned to us and said she needed to go up front and talk to the captain. I saw concern on her face—not a welcome sight at the end of a long day. The other flight attendant, Kim, and I just looked at each other, expecting the worst. It seemed like an eternity before Kelly returned and motioned for us to follow her to the front galley. As we did, I could tell the plane was circling in a holding pattern instead of making our normal descent.

"I've just been informed by the captain that we have a landing gear problem," Kelly said. "We need to prepare the cabin for an emergency landing."

As those words came out of her mouth, I felt like I was in a dream—or should I say a nightmare? But I remained calm and did my job. We discussed an emergency plan as the captain explained the situation over the intercom. You could have heard a pin drop as he clearly and distinctly spoke the words every passenger dreaded to hear.

"The problem," he said, "is that our indicator shows that the landing gear is not in the locked position for landing."

By this time, we knew what our next steps were, so we did what we had been trained to do.

The captain explained that he would do a "flyby" of the ATC Tower to see if they could confirm the status of the landing gear. He circled the plane close to the tower, but to our disappointment, they reported that it was too dark for them to see the undercarriage of the plane.

It was time to go over the emergency landing procedures with the passengers, which included instructing them in the brace position. We moved able and willing passengers to the window exit seats, then we went about securing the cabin. The sense of fear in the passengers became palpable as we conducted our final check and tried to reassure them. At one point, I glanced out at our intended runway and spotted a lineup of rescue vehicles and firetrucks. When landing gear failed to hold and an aircraft needed to "belly in" for the landing, it meant an increased risk of fire.

I sat in the front jump seat with Kelly as the cabin grew quiet and the plane descended. We held hands, and I prayed silently as the wheels hit the pavement. At such times, passengers watch the flight attendants' reactions closely, and because fear is contagious, we tried not to show our true feelings. Together, Kelly and I strained our ears as we listened for the reassuring sound of the wheels rolling—or the dire sound of metal sliding and scraping along the runway. It's hard to describe my sense of relief at the sweet sound of rolling wheels, which quickly brought the plane to smooth and full stop! The landing gear had held tight, and the passengers erupted into cheers and applause. The captain came on the PA system and confirmed that we were indeed safely on the ground.

Though exhausted, we began the deboarding procedures. As we said goodbye to the passengers, most of them thanked us for getting them to Roanoke safely. What might have been a disaster in the headlines turned instead into a scary what-might-have-been story.

I spoke with several concerned people in the airport terminal and then walked out to the parking lot with the other flight attendants. Family members hugged each other as survival stories were shared. I got into my car and just sat there, thinking about what had happened. I had been calm during the emergency, but now, safe in the front seat of my car, tears flowed down my cheeks. I thanked God for His mercies in keeping us all safe, then dried my eyes so that I could see well enough to drive home.

To this day, people ask me if incidents like that scared me enough to not want to fly again. I admit that incident made me feel apprehensive about flying my next trip, but my fear never grew strong enough to make me give up the job I loved.

Chapter 9

LEARNING

My first five years of flying for Piedmont Airlines were a real education for a small-town girl like me. Growing up, I had not been exposed to many different types of people, but as a working woman, I quickly learned never to bring up religion or politics with crews I did not know well. Those topics often led to long, potentially unpleasant discussions. I hailed from the Bible Belt, where what I believed and stood for was ingrained in me. My standards were tested at times, but the job gave me an opportunity to share and learn lessons along the way. I became aware that everyone has their own beliefs and that those beliefs are strongly influenced by how and where each person was raised. I had always felt blessed to grow up with Christian parents. The values I learned as a child stayed with me, and I was able to share my faith on many trips. I tried never to push my views on anyone, but I did lend a "listening ear" to my fellow crew members when they wanted to discuss problems. Those conversations often led to opportunities to share scripture or discuss how God helps in times of trouble.

From occasional confrontations with crew members or passengers, I learned the real meaning of the word "drama." But as a rule, I sought peace and worked hard to control how I reacted when challenged by a disgruntled person. Many times, I walked away instead of saying something I would regret, and I rarely regretted my decisions. When people entered the aircraft with burdens and problems from home, the flight attendants would often be the target of their bad day. It became a personal challenge for me to try to make disgruntled passengers smile before they left our flight. On many flights, passengers were traveling to funerals, visiting sick relatives, or feeling anxious about a job interview. I tried to keep that in mind when dealing with a passenger who seemed frustrated or upset.

I always hoped that my passengers deplaned feeling like they had been treated with fairness and kindness. I wanted them to be glad they flew with us and eager to fly with us again.

When I was hired in 1983 as a secretary for Piedmont, my idea of a flight attendant included the glamorous life and career portrayed by the media. But my perception changed after a few years of flying. While movies, television shows, and ads presented the role as a glitzy, easy job, they did not show details of the long hours spent sitting, waiting in airport terminals, and standing in hot airplane cabins while boarding. More times than I can count, we endured turbulent flights. It was definitely a job you had to love in order to succeed, especially given the time away from family, even on holidays. The job also involved a fair amount of risk. Hijackings, terrorist threats, and casualties could occur at any moment. Despite all that, I always thought that, given my personality, it was the best career for me. The job helped me grow as a person, and I learned something new in every city I visited.

As mentioned earlier, I had only flown once as an adult before becoming a flight attendant. Early on, I asked the pilots how such heavy aircraft could possibly lift off the ground on take-offs. The concept baffled me, even after taking off and landing thousands of times. Eventually, after multiple explanations, it made more sense to me— something to do with pressure and air flow—but don't ask me for details! All I knew—and still know—is that air travel is the safest and quickest way to get to your destination.

Keep those seat belts fastened to learn a lot more about the wonders of flying. The world of aviation is fascinating!

Part II

USAIR

"When once you have tasted flight, you will
forever walk the earth with your eyes
turned skyward, for there you have been,
and there you will always long to return."

~ Leonardo DaVinci

Chapter 10

CELEBRITIES

The news hit the papers on March 9, 1987, that USAir Group, Inc. offered a $1.59 billion deal to buy Piedmont Aviation, Inc. We were relieved because we finally knew our working fate, and all of the speculations of the past months were put to rest. The merger would create the nation's seventh-largest airline because USAir was also in the process of acquiring Pacific Southwest Airlines, which serviced the western states. Ultimately, the combined assets of the three airlines would become US Airways.

In the late 1980s and early 1990s, it was not unusual to encounter celebrities on our flights because they often flew out of Los Angeles or New York. Some of these well-known people stood out among the others.

The actor Richard Gere boarded one of our flights out of LaGuardia, New York, on his way to Charlotte, North Carolina. He was performing on Broadway at the time, and I was at the boarding door when he was suddenly standing right in front of me. I probably blushed as I spoke to him, as it was such a shock to see him in person. He had purchased three seats in the back of the plane and wanted nothing more than to lie down and get some sleep.

"If you can get me a couple pillows and a blanket," he said quietly, "I will be all set."

I asked him which seats he had and told him I would be back in a few minutes with his requests. As I walked away, I made a stop in the lavatory to get my composure back. That may sound crazy, but he had been one of my favorite actors ever since I watched the 1982 movie *An Officer and a Gentleman*, so I was a bit flustered.

I took his pillow and blanket with me to his row in the back, but when I got there, he was already out like a light. I placed the items on the aisle seat and reluctantly walked away. I had wanted to ask a couple of questions of him because when else would I have the opportunity to look into the face of one of my favorite actors? But alas, better that he get the rest he needed. When I returned to the back galley to start our service, the other flight attendants were full of questions and wanted to know everything he had said. I wished I had something more exciting to tell them other than, "Get me a couple of pillows and a blanket."

My favorite Hollywood "gentleman" slept for the entire flight, and the only word I heard from him later was "Goodbye" as he exited the plane.

A few months later, Tom Cruise flew with us to Los Angeles, accompanied by his wife at the time, Mimi Rogers. They sat in first class and were both friendly and chatty. I had a nice conversation with them. Tom surprised me with his congeniality, especially when he walked to the front galley and spoke with us during the flight.

Donald Trump was on one of my flights to West Palm

Beach, and never in a thousand years did I imagine I was serving a meal to the future US president! He and his then wife, Marla Maples, were sitting in first class, and I even remarked to the other flight attendant how friendly he was. He asked me where I lived and how long I had been a flight attendant. Most celebrities sit quietly and don't want to be disturbed, but not him. He seemed to have a real interest in aviation too, because I did not know then that he had started his own airline in 1989 called the Trump Shuttle. Interestingly enough, US Airways acquired it in 1992, and I flew with several of his former employees.

The singer Lee Greenwood boarded our flight from Charlotte to Atlanta, before which we had an Air Traffic Control (ATC) delay. After we'd been waiting an hour for takeoff, I asked him to sing "God Bless the USA" for us, but he only laughed and said his guitar was checked and stored underneath the airplane. When I told him it would sure make the delay more pleasant, he chuckled and said he would sing if we all sang backup for him. I think he was surprised when I agreed. I made the announcement that Lee Greenwood was on our flight and had agreed to treat us to a song. I held the microphone as we all sang together, and a long delay was made a little less boring. Meanwhile, Mr. Greenwood surely gained a few new fans that day!

One night, I worked with another flight attendant on an F-28 aircraft, which is a small fifty-seat jet. It was late and we had a full flight from Greensboro to Charlotte, both in North Carolina. In Greensboro, we hurriedly boarded the passengers so that we could finish our final flight for the night. As I welcomed everyone, I noticed what I thought was a familiar face, so I asked the passenger in question if he was Steven Spielberg. The other flight attendant, Bill, looked at me like I might be crazy.

"I wish I had a dollar for every time someone asks me that," the passenger said.

"You sure look like him," I said, "but then again, I've heard that everyone has a double!"

"I only wish I had his money," he said with a laugh.

Bill whispered to me that he did not think that was him.

"But he's wearing the jean shirt and cap he always wears," I insisted.

"Then why would he be traveling on our flight out of Greensboro and sitting in coach class?"

I had to admit that was a good question.

Even though the flight was only twenty-five minutes long, we began our refreshment service.

"Steven," I said when I got to the man's seat, "what would you like to drink?"

"Just a coke," he said with a grin.

Later, after Bill spoke with the Spielberg doppelganger, he approached me excitedly. "That *is* Steven Spielberg!" he exclaimed. "He stopped me on my way up the aisle and told me he was Steven but not to tell you. He said he was having too much fun."

"See?" I said. "I don't remember names, but I never forget faces!"

I smiled at the famous director as the passengers deplaned. "I knew it was you," I said.

He turned and flicked his eyebrows up. "Sometimes it's fun being someone else."

There were many other celebrities on my flights, but those were some of the favorites that stood out among the rest. Most turned out to be friendly but simply wanted to be left alone. And I tried never to draw attention to them as it might create a stir in the cabin with passengers asking questions. Today, many celebrities fly on their own jets. Gone are the days when they depended on commercial travel to get them to their destinations, but I'm sure there are still some lucky flight attendants meeting their matinee idols now and again.

Chapter 11

NATURE

Snow and Ice

There are not many industries as affected by bad weather as the aviation business. Back in 1987, I was on a Boeing 737-200 heading to Charleston, West Virginia, in a severe snowstorm. As the heavy aircraft landed and the brakes were applied, I felt the wheels slide one way and then the other several times. Sitting on the back jump seat, I heard screams as passengers didn't know whether we might slide off the runway next. A few minutes later, sighs of relief filled the cabin as people realized we had safely stopped.

After deplaning the passengers, I peeked outside and noticed the pounding snow reducing visibility by the minute. Air Traffic Control (ATC) let us know that the airport was closed and that we were the last plane to land that day. Obviously, our flight out was cancelled, so we called scheduling to find out what our next move should be. With an airport closure, the crew has limited choices, and we were told we'd need to work the first flight out the next morning. We called the hotel and were picked up by their shuttle service, but the roads were so treacherous that it took two hours to get there. Needless to say, I didn't get much sleep that night.

The ride back to the airport the next morning was almost as long. We arrived at 6:00 a.m. only to find out that the flight was delayed two hours, which meant two hours to find something to do; sleep is what I wanted to do! Most of us decided to eat breakfast and then board the aircraft. While eating, I overheard a conversation that I wished I hadn't. The captain and first officer were discussing how it was the first officer's inaugural trip on a 737-200, and here, in Charleston, it was his turn to take off. He seemed a little nervous as he talked about the conditions. I turned to the other two flight attendants, who had also been listening, and we all stared at each other with concern. Let me just say, our pilots are very well trained and have many hours of experience under their belt before they're allowed in the cockpit, but after sliding on the runway the previous evening, we all felt anxious about the takeoff. And it didn't help that the Charleston airport sat atop a hill with a sharp three-hundred-foot drop on all sides.

We boarded the full plane for a nonstop flight to Greensboro, North Carolina. As the fumes of the deicing fluid filled the crowded cabin, I thought about how we would be the first plane to take off after the airport closure. I quickly did the final cabin check and took my seat in the back galley. I was alone and kept flashing back to the conversation between the pilots; I couldn't help but picture the high cliffs surrounding the airport and how one wrong turn could spell disaster.

I glanced out the small round window on the back door

to see how the runway looked: still icy and covered with snow. As the engine grew louder, my fingers tightened around the edge of the jump seat, my anxiety peaking. The aircraft rolled faster on the pavement, and I said a short prayer. God had kept me safe so far in my life, and I asked Him to please do the same now. As the airplane's wheels lifted off the pavement, I felt like shouting with glee, but the passengers beat me to it with their claps and cheers. Clearly, they had been anxious too, but everyone breathed a collective sigh of relief as we left the snowy runway behind and flew toward the wispy clouds. The sunshine helped eliminate any remaining jitters, and memories of ice and snow melted away.

Tornado

In 1991, we landed in Kansas City, Missouri, and had an hour on the ground before reboarding for Charlotte. We taxied to the gate and deplaned the full flight. Catherine, the other flight attendant, and I decided to leave the plane to grab dinner. As we stood in line for our food, we heard a page for the crew of flight 1652 to return to the aircraft immediately. We stepped out of line and hurried back to the gate. The male agent who'd made the announcement opened the door for us to return down the jetway to the aircraft.

"We're getting ready to announce an emergency evacuation," he said as he closed the door.

We rushed to the entryway of the plane to find the captain standing inside. "If you look out the window on the right side," he said, "you'll see why we called you back."

Catherine and I looked out and saw the threat. In the

distance, a dark, funnel-type formation was barreling toward us—a tornado! It was probably several miles away, but we didn't want to take any chances and be in the boarding process if it hit the airport. The captain told us to get our belongings because we'd all be sheltering in the basement area of the terminal. We retrieved our bags and headed for the door. As we passed the first-class windows, I glanced outside and saw the funnel getting closer. Meanwhile, the ground crew outside was tying down the aircraft, hoping to keep it free of damage.

Once back in the terminal, I saw a line of people at the elevator and stairways. The evacuation announcement had been made, and people wore looks of fear on their faces. My only other tornado experience was when I camped in Oklahoma as a child. We'd heard a loud buzzer and a message detailing that we were under the threat of a tornado. My family was in a tent, which was obviously no match for the high winds and twists and turns of such a powerful force. We evacuated to an underground shelter and stayed there for several hours. Luckily, the tornado missed our campground, and we were able to enjoy the evening unharmed.

Now, years later, here I was doing the same thing. We clambered down the stairs with everyone else to a cement-walled, windowless area, and I wondered how long we would need to hunker down. Outside, the wind whistled, and carts and machinery knocked against the building. I could only imagine the damage the tornado might cause. An hour later, the tornado turned and spared the airport but unfortunately ended up tearing through Wichita, Kansas. We were told to return to the aircraft, and after a delay of several hours, we boarded the flight and made it safely to Charlotte.

Sadly, we later learned that the tornado had killed seventeen people in Wichita and injured 225. It also did 62 million dollars' worth of damage to McConnell Air Force Base.

Earthquakes

Most of you probably remember hearing of the tragedy in San Francisco on October 17, 1989—the Loma Prieta earthquake that struck the San Francisco Bay Area. It killed sixty-three people and injured 3,757 others. I was not there that day, but I arrived a week later for a layover. On the way to the hotel that night, our van driver told us that the 6.9 magnitude quake had not only destroyed multiple buildings at the Marina—where I often walked and enjoyed fresh seafood—but that the San Francisco–Oakland Bay Bridge was also damaged when a piece of the top deck collapsed.

Asleep at the hotel that night, I was startled awake by the sound of ice shaking in the glass beside my bed. I thought I was dreaming at first but then realized it was an aftershock from the earthquake. We had been warned that we might feel unusual shaking in the area, but I really did not expect it. I lay there wondering if I should call downstairs or evacuate the building. My room was on the twelfth floor, and I sure didn't want to be there if another temblor struck. I decided that I'd call if I still felt movement in an hour, which I didn't, so I wrote it off to aftershocks and tried to sleep. The next day, I met some of the crew to have breakfast. As we climbed the hill to the restaurant, the conversation turned to the previous night's shakes, and we all agreed it would be a relief to head back home in a few hours.

On June 15, 2004, I had a nice, long layover in San Diego, California. After a morning of visiting Sea Port Village, which was close to our hotel downtown, a few of us enjoyed lunch at a waterfront restaurant. I always appreciated the perfect weather in San Diego and often took the ferry to Coronado Beach, but not that day. I had flown two trips in a row to complete the required hours for my monthly obligation, so I shopped for a few hours after lunch and then returned to my room to rest before working the red-eye that night. It was 3:30 p.m. local time, and I had just closed the dark curtains when I felt a sudden shake. At first, I thought one of the large cruise ships on the waterfront had moved. I looked out the window to see if I was correct, but the two ships were still anchored where they had been. As I walked toward my bed, I felt another big tremble, so I called the front desk and asked if we were having an earthquake and if I needed to evacuate. The clerk answered in a very passive voice: "Yes, we are having an earthquake, but at this time, you don't need to leave your room."

I turned on the television and learned that a 5.3 magnitude earthquake was occurring offshore near Baja, California. I debated whether to remain in my room and decided to try and rest but keep the news report going. Apparently, there were no significant damages throughout the area. Once again, I had survived one of the earth's surprises, but I was safe and even slept a few hours before flying home that night.

With all the challenges I experienced through thirty-four years of flying, I knew who was ultimately in control of these extreme weather conditions. I knew God Almighty could calm the storms and winds, and that He held me safely in his hands. That doesn't mean I didn't feel fear at times, but I knew He was by my side each and every moment during the storms in my life.

Chapter 12

MOVING

It was a sad day around the Piedmont system when all of the base closings were announced. Since Roanoke was one of those bases, we learned that most of our flight attendants would be transferred to Charlotte, Baltimore, or Greensboro. We could either move to another base or adjust to the life of a commuter. Given my divorce, I decided the best option for my daughter and me was to move to Charlotte.

In the summer of 1989, we packed up and moved to a townhouse thirty minutes from the airport. It was a big step because I had lived in Roanoke all my life. Once settled, the most important factor became finding a dependable sitter for my daughter, and I went through several before finding a reliable one. Only a month after moving, Amanda and I endured Hurricane Hugo, a new experience for us because Roanoke had been protected from such natural events by the Blue Ridge Mountains. Hugo took portions of my roof with him, and we lived without electricity for over a month. The once-beautiful streets of Charlotte looked like a war zone after Hugo passed through.

On a cold winter night in January of 1990, I returned home from a three-day trip to see a car in my usual parking spot behind my townhouse, so I found a place in the lower end of the lot. Amanda was staying with my next-door neighbor, so I went over and visited for a while. Then Amanda and I went home and got ready for bed. I was exhausted, so it only took a few minutes to fall asleep. Hours later, a loud noise startled me awake. I sleepily squinted at my alarm clock: 3:40 a.m. Was I having a dream, or did I really hear a big thud? Had Amanda fallen down the stairs?

I ran to her room and found her asleep, but as I returned to my room, I heard muffled voices downstairs. I darted into my bedroom and picked up the only "weapon" I could find: my tennis racket!

My heart pounded as I crept to the phone and dialed 911. I whispered to the dispatcher that someone had broken into my house. She told me to remain on the phone and that help would arrive in a few minutes.

I dropped the phone on my bed and headed toward Amanda's room. I did not want anything to happen to her if the intruders came upstairs. As I slammed and locked her bedroom door, I screamed out, "Who's there?"

I really did not expect an answer, but I wanted them to know I was upstairs. Perhaps they had thought the house was empty because I hadn't parked in my usual spot.

Then I pushed the chest of drawers in front of the door, explaining the situation to Amanda in a panicked whisper. Without hesitation, I dashed to the window and removed the screen, telling Amanda that we needed to make our escape through the window and drop onto the storage building. But before we could, two men skedaddled out of my back door and disappeared into the darkness. They wore hooded jackets, so I never did get a look at them.

After the police arrived, I learned that the intruders had broken in through my kitchen door and had gathered my few valuables on the kitchen table. I must have scared them off when I yelled, though I doubt they would have run off so fast had they known I only had a tennis racket as a weapon! Once again, I gave thanks to God that we did not get robbed or hurt that night; however, I did go home to Virginia the next weekend to learn how to shoot a gun. I still have my concealed carry permit today. After a scare like that, you become a lighter sleeper and feel a bit more comfort knowing you are protected.

In the spring of 1990, I worked a flight to San Diego. When we landed, the captain told me that he had been notified by scheduling that my daughter was in the Presbyterian Hospital in Charlotte. I was to call the nurse in the emergency room to get more information. "They have removed you from this trip," he said. This incident happened in the days before cell phones were everywhere, so I was anxious to get to a payphone in the airport terminal. It seemed like an eternity before we arrived at the gate and I was able to deplane.

I learned from a nurse that Amanda had fallen during gym class and broken her collarbone, and they needed my authorization to treat her. On the flight home, I decided to move back to Roanoke because in Charlotte, Amanda was without family while I was traveling. The distance from immediate family had simply become too difficult a situation to manage, and the accumulation of negative events made my decision easier. God evidently wanted me back in Virginia for several reasons, but I wondered why I had felt so sure about my decision to move to Charlotte a year earlier.

Sometimes God teaches us lessons in hardship. While living away from Virginia and family, I felt like I had battled one problem after another. In addition, I'd never found a church in the year I lived there, and my spiritual life had suffered. I felt in my heart that the best decision for us was to move back to Roanoke. Only God knew why our life elsewhere had not seemed to work out.

Within weeks, we packed our belongings and headed back to Virginia, where I continue to live. It ultimately turned out to be a good decision because it provided a more stable life for my daughter and led to the wonderful marriage I enjoy today. Once back, I bought a house and decided not to complain about commuting again. It worked for a while!

To fly more international trips, I transferred to the base in Philadelphia. But after six months of commuting from Roanoke to Philadelphia, the "hop" became more than I could bear. Unfortunately, I was unable to switch back to Charlotte as my base for another two years, so I endured the inconvenience.

I learned as I got older, however, to make decisions based on what makes life easier and more manageable. Commuting to Charlotte made my life easier because I had the option of driving. There are very few jobs that allow an employee to work in one state or country and live in another! Flight attendants commute from all over the United

States and from countries as far away as Europe. It may bring on more anxiety, but that is when you ask yourself if it's worth it. For me, it always was.

Chapter 13

CATASTROPHE

On the evening of February 1, 1991, USAir Flight 1493, a Boeing 737-300, collided with SkyWest Flight 5569, a Metro-liner turboprop aircraft. The collision occurred upon landing at the Los Angeles International Airport. Although air traffic had not been any busier than usual at LAX, the local air traffic controller evidently had several distractions, and he made the mistake of instructing the SkyWest plane to take off on the same runway where the Boeing intended to land.

I was in the kitchen cooking dinner around 5:00 p.m. when a news alert came on the television. It caught my attention because as I watched the footage of the crash site, I noticed the tail number of the 737. I found the logbook in which I recorded my flights and flipped through it. Sure enough, I had flown on that same plane two weeks earlier. I got chills knowing that I could have been in that accident, but that is the reality that flight attendants keep in the back of their minds. While our job is thought to be adventurous, the truth is that we are all just one landing away from disaster. In order to enjoy such a career, it is important not to dwell too long on such realities.

I turned off the stove and sat in front of the television to listen to the report.

"USAir Flight 1493 originated in Syracuse, New York," said the reporter. "With a stop in Port Columbus International Airport, the flight flew on to Los Angeles, and the crash occurred on landing."

It was later reported that there were eighty-three passengers and six crew members aboard Flight 1493. Of that number, twenty-three fatalities and twenty-nine injuries were reported. I could have been one of them. The SkyWest flight 5569 had ten passengers and two crew members, all of whom were killed. It took me a few days to shake off a profound feeling of sadness, and my thoughts stayed preoccupied with the flight attendants involved and the families of the crew and passengers who were lost.

I later discovered that even if we aren't physically involved in a crash, we can experience PTSD after hearing about a life-threatening situation because we think, What if...?

I compare it to survivor's guilt, in which a survivor feels guilty for being alive while people they knew or worked with did not survive. One of the crew members who survived the LAX collision was my friend Bill Ibarra. He was one of the flight attendants, and he shared his remarkable story at a 2017 conference I attended. He suffered smoke inhalation and second-degree burns when the aircraft caught on fire. Then he spent nineteen days in the ICU on a ventilator. In total, he remained in the hospital for forty-five days.

I wondered how someone could continue to endure the pain and memories of such an experience and still fly. But he mentioned that he made it a point never to talk about that tragic time because he preferred to dwell on the positive things in his life rather than the negative. After he physically recovered from the accident, Bill continued his career with US Airways. His biggest internal battle became forgiving the air traffic controller who had made the mistake, but he was eventually able to do it with God's help. Today, Bill helps others as part of the Critical Incident Response Team, a group I will provide more information on in a later chapter. He is able to do such noble work because he has a positive attitude about life and knows he was given a second chance to make a difference in the world.

Thank you, Bill, for all you do to help others!

Chapter 14

LEG

By the tenth year of my flying career with USAir, much had changed. We had a new base and new training procedures, but in spite of all that, one thing had not changed: the word "flexible." We had all learned that flexibility is vital in the life of a flight attendant. For example, a simple three-day trip can turn into a four-day trip if there are weather or mechanical problems. One afternoon, I found myself running through the Philadelphia airport with other crew members because we had arrived late due to weather and air traffic problems. We were slated to fly to Orlando, Florida, on a large Boeing 757, where I was to work the back section. We made it just in time.

The plane was completely full, a very common occurrence with Florida destinations. For pre-boarding, I was standing at my position beside the 3R door—the third door on the right—when a middle-aged woman with two grown children entered the aircraft. The man immediately behind them wore shorts, which revealed his prosthetic leg. I approached him and asked if I could be of any assistance.

He said that he and his family were fine, so I assured him that I would be nearby if they needed me. He nodded and thanked me, but after they were seated, he stretched his artificial leg out across the middle aisle.

The first-class passengers began boarding, and after them, we would board the coach passengers.

"Sir," I whispered to him, "you really need to move your leg out of the aisle." He looked at me and told me his leg would not bend. "It's a new leg," he said, "and something has happened to the spring that allows the knee to bend." He seemed embarrassed by the predicament, so I asked him to follow me to the rear lavatory so that we could find a solution to the problem.

He entered the bathroom and locked the door but did not come out again, even after ten or fifteen minutes had passed.

I knocked on the door. "Sir, how are you doing?"

Once he heard my voice, he cracked open the door and told me he was not having any success in getting his knee to bend. I asked him to come out; he did, sweating and out of breath.

"Where is the spring located?" I asked. He pointed to his thigh area, so I leaned down and tried to find the latch. By that time, I was feeling foolish and could feel the stares of the passengers seated around us, but after considerable effort, I still couldn't fix the problem.

"Sir, you have two choices. You can take a later flight once you get your leg fixed or you can take your leg off." Before I even finished speaking, he reached down, took off his leg, and handed it to me. I found myself standing in the aisle holding a prosthetic leg with a white size-thirteen tennis shoe dangling off the end. The passenger deftly maneuvered down the aisle and took his seat while I stood in place. People never seem to miss an opportunity to laugh when they see an unusual situation and have nothing else to do. I needed to find a place to put the leg… and fast.

All of this happened during the boarding process. As the other flight attendants were closing bins in preparation for takeoff, I tried to help—all the while holding the leg in my right hand. People snickered and pointed at me as I walked past the rows, but I'm sure my discomfort was nothing compared to situations the man endured every day. I finally found a bin over row 9 that would accommodate the limb, and as I put it in there out of sight, the passengers around me clapped. I walked back to the owner of the leg and told him where I had put it.

"Thank you," he said. "I'll try to have it fixed before our flight home." He had already told me they were on their way to Disney World.

"You'd better get your leg fixed before you go see Mickey Mouse."

He laughed and said he would definitely do that.

After we landed, another flight attendant asked what in the world I had been doing, and after I explained the situation, she shook her head and said, "Only you." I have to admit, I always seemed to attract unusual situations in the air!

Chapter 15

LATE

In 1995, I enjoyed a little more seniority and was able to bid and hold some trips that I loved. During a trip to San Francisco, one of my favorite west coast destinations, I got to attend a party. My friend lived in the small town of Saratoga, and she invited me to a birthday party for her twin sons. I arranged a red-eye trip with a twenty-eight-hour layover that gave me enough time to go, plus it would add to my hours for the month.

We flight attendants usually signed up for our hours by bidding on a block or a line of trips, and US Air allowed us to fly as many hours as we wanted, as long as the total fell between fifty and one hundred twenty. I chose to fly eighty to eighty-five hours per month, over twelve to fifteen days. People always thought it was a great schedule, and it was, but they seldom considered that we were only paid for the actual hours in the air. When we landed and the doors opened, the clock stopped, although we did get a small hourly allowance that helped pay for food during layovers.

We arrived in San Francisco at 8:00 p.m., and I handed

the lead flight attendant my contact information in case they needed me, which was the customary thing to do for those who didn't plan to go to the hotel with the rest of the crew. As soon as the passengers deplaned, I rented a car and made the one-hour drive to Saratoga, where I spent the night with my friends. The small town was so pretty, and they had the birthday party the next day, which was all the more enjoyable because despite it being winter, it was warm and sunny in California. My flight was scheduled to leave at ten that night, so I wanted to get back to the airport in plenty of time for my departure.

I arrived at 7:30 p.m., which gave me time to freshen up and be ready to board the plane at nine, but when I got to the gate, the agent informed me that the aircraft was delayed and would not arrive until midnight. She also told me that scheduling had called my crew, who'd elected to stay at the hotel. She must have noticed my disappointment because she suggested I go to the old crew room and take a nap. I was tired and thought that was a great idea! Before walking away, I turned to the agent and asked her to make sure the flight crew knew where I would be. She nodded that she understood, and I saw her write it down.

I took the escalator to the second floor and found the quiet room. A few of my fellow flight attendants were sleeping on various couches, and as I searched for my alarm clock, I heard a voice from the other side of the couch.

"What time do you need to get up?"

"In two hours," I said.

"I have mine set for that time too," came the reply from the friendly companion. "I'll wake you up before I leave."

I thought that was really nice of her and that perhaps we

were on the same flight. In a few minutes, I drifted off to sleep. When I finally woke up, I found myself alone in the big dark room, with the only light coming from the drink machines. I used them to illuminate my watch and was horrified to see that it was 1:30 a.m.!

"Oh no!" I shouted. Where was the sweet girl who assured me she would wake me up? Who turned out all the lights?

I gathered my belongings, and without even checking my appearance, I ran to the escalator, where I proceeded to fall on the first two steps and tear my pantyhose. Barely managing to avoid a fall down the rest of the stairs, I reached the gate out of breath and discombobulated.

"I'm the flight attendant who was supposed to work the flight back to Charlotte!" I exclaimed to the agent behind the counter.

"I'm sorry," she said, "but that flight left forty-five minutes ago."

I felt dizzy as I considered the consequences of missing a flight. "How could they leave without me? Were they looking for me?"

"I think they made a call or two about you."

"Where is the original agent who was boarding the flight?"

"She got off at eleven."

I began to cry and tried to explain what had happened. "They probably thought I didn't make it back to the airport."

I later learned that my friends from Saratoga had searched the highways when they received a call from my crew members. I can't imagine what must have been going through their minds, so I got in touch to reassure them. Then, with my heart pounding in fear, I called scheduling and told them I was the missing flight attendant from Flight 5043.

"We didn't know you weren't on that flight," a male scheduler said.

"What?" I cried out.

"Now that we know you didn't work the flight, we'll have to write you up for this."

Wow, I'd just told on myself.

"Well, I'm still here in San Francisco," I said, "so can you put me on the next flight back to Charlotte please?"

What a night! What had seemed to be a good idea ended up being a nightmare! I took the escalator back up to the crew room and fell asleep on the same couch, this time remembering to set my alarm. As I lay there thinking about what happened, I thought it was odd that the original gate agent did not tell the crew where I was, especially since she knew her shift ended at eleven. And my earlier couch-neighbor hadn't bothered to wake me up. I never did learn the reason for either lapse.

When I arrived in Charlotte, I met with my supervisor. She took one look at me and said, "I believe you had a rough night!"

I laughed and admitted I was upset with myself and the situation. She looked at my "dependability records" and noticed that this was my first mishap.

"I think you've learned your lesson," she said. "So as far as I'm concerned, you don't need any discipline."

I was beyond happy not to get fired or receive a disciplinary letter in my file that might later lead to consequences. And I was so grateful when I learned that my flight crew had not reported me as missing because they hadn't wanted me to get into trouble. Since they had the required number of attendants on board, they thought it better to go ahead without relaying my mistake. Nice crew!

You live and learn. I'm sure everyone reading this has been in a similar situation. Ultimately, no one I depended on that night did what they said they would do, so from that point on, I always set my own alarms before my flights. Lessons are valuable to accumulate in life, but they are not always easy to acquire!

Part III

US AIRWAYS

"Sometimes, flying feels too God-like to be attained by man. Sometimes, the world from above seems too beautiful, too wonderful, too distant for human eyes to see."

~ Charles A. Lindbergh

Chapter 16

MONKEY

I was flying some island trips now and enjoying the change of scenery and different crews I flew with. On this trip, I was flying out of Miami on the Boeing 757 and working in the back during boarding. Given that we were in Florida, most passengers wore shorts and tank tops. Whenever I traveled through tropical locations, I would get a desire to plan my next vacation. Who wouldn't? Warm sunny weather was always appealing when the weather at home was dreary and cold.

As boarding continued, I noticed a young man take a seat in the rear exit row. I thought it was strange that as hot as it was on our plane and outside, he wore a jacket. We finished boarding and closed all the bins and completed the flight safety demonstration, then I took my jump seat in the back. I talked to the passengers in front of me, including the young man with the heavy jacket, who avoided making eye contact. The lady beside him was sharing the fabulous details of her recent cruise and barely catching a breath between words.

As I listened to this talkative passenger, the young man pressed on the front of his jacket. I asked him where he had been. He told me he was on his way home from South America.

"I've never been there," I said.

He looked uncomfortable as he shifted back and forth in his seat. I decided to observe his behavior closely as I sensed something wasn't right, and I just couldn't understand why he was wearing such a heavy jacket.

A few more minutes passed, and then I noticed the front of the man's jacket moving, but he wasn't touching it. The jacket had moved by itself! Either he had something in there or he had a serious case of indigestion.

The seat belt sign turned off, indicating we had reached our cruising altitude, and I needed to address the "moving jacket" issue. I walked over and leaned down to whisper in his ear. "What do you have under your jacket?"

He turned to me. "Why are you asking?"

I told him I had noticed something moving that I assumed wasn't his stomach.

He sheepishly looked at me. "If I show you, are you going to turn me in?"

I studied his face and replied, "I guess that depends on what it is."

At that moment, he unzipped the jacket to reveal a cute little monkey's face. I could hardly believe what I was seeing! I had thought maybe he was carrying a puppy or a kitten, but not a monkey! I gasped and placed my hand on my mouth. The lady beside him did the same. He explained that he had gotten this far with the monkey and begged me not to tell. I have a soft heart for animals, but at the same time, I knew this small animal was not permitted in the United States without papers. I shook my head at the man and walked away.

I had no choice but to report this to the captain. When we arrived in Philadelphia, the passenger was met by security. I had to write up a lengthy report concerning the incident, and I actually never heard what consequences the man paid for illegally transporting an animal. Nor did I find out what happened to the little monkey.

When I later discussed the incident with my supervisor, she asked me how I noticed it. I told her I have an inquisitive mind, love a good mystery, and tend to notice details. Obviously, the first clue was the heavy jacket on a really hot day!

"Good traits to have in this business," she said. And I knew that to be true because it paid off more than once in figuring out mysterious passengers.

Chapter 17

TURBULENCE

Flight attendants dislike turbulence as much as the passengers. Most air disturbances are caused by weather conditions such as thunderstorms, but they can also be caused by the jet streams of large aircraft. These are called Clear Air Turbulence (CAT) and can stretch for thousands of miles and be a few miles in depth. CAT can be so unexpected and dramatic that it can throw a person who is not securely seated all the way to the ceiling of the plane. I had heard many flight attendants tell horror stories of being in CAT, but I had not yet experienced it.

Most of the time, pilots knew the weather ahead of time and would warn the flight attendants of the probability of a bad weather pattern. They would also do their best to fly around the disturbances, but it wasn't always possible.

We found ourselves in a dangerous situation on a flight from Charlotte to Birmingham, Alabama. We had a partially full flight on a Boeing 737-200, which seated around 120 passengers. I was the "B" flight attendant working the back of the aircraft. With forty minutes left until landing, we tended to our end-of-flight duties, some of which were to dump the coffee, restock the carts, and re-ice the beer and wine. These were simple tasks on most flights, but during our approach to Birmingham, we hit Clear Air Turbulence.

I was bending down to ice the beer kit but wasn't holding onto a secure object. Suddenly, we dropped in altitude, and everything around me flew to the floor. Canned drinks exploded, and I lost my balance as my body slammed into the galley counter. In the lavatory, a woman screamed, and I could hear the sound of objects falling in there. A call from the cockpit told us to get to our jump seats and strap in, but I stopped to knock on the lavatory door to ask the passenger if she was okay.

"Yes, just a little scared and rattled!"

I knew what she meant, and I told her to stay where she was and to hold onto something until the turbulence subsided. I looked up the aisle and saw a downed flight attendant trying to stand. As I slowly made my way to her, I maintained my balance by holding onto the edges of the aisle seats. When I got closer, I saw that her leg was twisted awkwardly behind her. No way would she be able to stand.

"I think I broke my leg," she said. As I turned to go back to the phone to call the cockpit, I felt pain in my right rib area. I told the captain we had both been injured and had lost contact with the "A" flight attendant in the front of the aircraft. He said he would declare a medical emergency landing and that we should get the cabin ready.

Everywhere I looked, people had spilled drinks on themselves, and several of the overhead bins had opened, allowing bags to fall out and block the aisle. I tried to lift several pieces of luggage in order to make my way to the front galley but was unable to because of my injury. The pain grew worse, and it was all I could do to endure it until I reached the front. Once there, I found Kathy sitting on the floor, holding her arm.

"I think it's broken," she cried. I assured her that we were making our descent and told her that Reneé had broken her leg. At that moment, I realized I was the healthiest of the three flight attendants on board.

I called the cockpit again and informed them that we all needed medical attention once we reached the gate at Birmingham. The captain estimated eighteen minutes before we would be on the ground. I decided it would be best for me to sit on the front door jump seat so I could get the exit door opened more easily.

Glancing at the passenger list, I noticed there were two people on board who were airline employees. I asked them to assist me in moving the other flight attendants to empty first-class seats. Then I asked one of them to sit on the back jump seat as we landed and to disarm the slides at each door. It was my only choice, and although this was an unusual situation, it was necessary for me to use whoever was available to help with what needed to be done.

I took my seat but could hardly strap the belt around my body because of the shooting pain in my chest. Something inside of me was injured, probably my ribs. We taxied to the gate, and the captain called to ask how we were doing. I told him what I had done, and he agreed it was the best solution to make sure both exits were covered on landing.

Sirens screamed out as we got closer to the terminal, and once we were at the gate, I cracked open the front door. To my relief, I saw several medical responders waiting for us.

Although no passengers had mentioned any injuries, I made the announcement that if anyone was hurt, they should check with the medical personnel as they deplaned. Luckily, most of the passengers had secured their seatbelts, except for the poor lady in the bathroom. Although she did ask for medical help, she turned out not to be injured.

The other flight attendants and I were transported to the local emergency room, where I was diagnosed with three broken ribs. Kathy and Reneé were treated for broken limbs, but we all felt fortunate that we had not been more severely injured.

The moral of the story? Keep your seatbelt fastened while on flights. As we always say, unexpected turbulence is no friend to anyone!

Chapter 18

CORK

The name change from USAir to US Airways came with a new color scheme and updated aircraft designs. The new color schemes used red, white, and blue with our new logo, which was the US Airways flag on the tail of each aircraft. It was a beautiful sight after years of old colors and a mixture of different logos with all the mergers. The interiors were updated to dark navy leather, and we received a lot of positive response from our passengers.

Around that time, I was flying a three-day trip on the Boeing 737-200, and my last layover was in Montreal, Canada. I loved the city of Montreal and enjoyed the sights and shopping there.

"Have you ever seen our black squirrels?" the van driver asked. The drivers often gave us mini-tours on the way to our hotel, and this man seemed to enjoy pointing out differences between Canada and the United States, e.g., the local foods, the typical cold weather, and interesting details about the animals. The crew normally wanted to know about good places to shop and eat, and we often rated the layovers by those two factors.

I was the lead flight attendant on this trip, and as I was busy boarding the flight from Montreal to Charlotte, one of the first-class passengers asked for a mimosa, but I informed her that I was not allowed to open our liquor kits while we were still on the ground because of international rules. I reassured her that I would get her the drink once we were airborne. I sat down on the forward jump seat beside the "C" flight attendant and asked her to remind me to ice a bottle of champagne. We talked about our layover and the fun we had had exploring the little shops in Montreal and eating at one of the local restaurants.

Once we leveled off, I started my service. I put the champagne on ice and served everyone except the lady in 2F. I told her I would have her drink ready in a few minutes. I went back to the galley and lifted the bottle out of the cooler. It was still in the drawer but high enough for me to remove the cork. Unfortunately, as I did, the cork flew out like a ball that had been shot from a cannon. It smacked me right in the eye, and I felt such a sharp pain that I wondered if my eye had been knocked out of its socket. With my remaining good eye, I looked on the floor to make sure it wasn't there because I was afraid I might step on it! I know that sounds crazy, but I think I was in a state of shock.

I called the cockpit immediately. "I've been hit by a cork!" I exclaimed to the captain.

"Say again?"

I explained as best I could, trying not to cry. He said he'd send out the first officer and then call MedLink, our resource for medical emergencies.

I was standing in the galley with ice on my possibly

empty eye socket when the officer came out.

"Watch where you're walking!" I screamed. "I think the cork knocked my eye out." He asked me to lower the towel and let him see what damage had been done. With much trepidation and pain, I opened my eyelid for him. "Is it still there?" I asked nervously.

"It sure is, but it's totally red, and you may have torn your retina."

I heaved a sigh of relief. At least my body part was still visible and intact.

The captain came on the intercom and announced an emergency medical landing in Philadelphia. Then he called me and said I would be transported by the rescue squad to the Wills Eye Hospital. I got one of the other flight attendants to finish the service in first class, and I stayed seated for the remainder of the flight. In Philadelphia, I would be replaced by another flight attendant.

Once we got to the gate, I opened the front aircraft door and was met by three medics and a base supervisor, who handed me her card and told me to call if I needed anything. At the hospital, I was told I had a partially detached retina and a hematoma, so they put a patch on the eye and recommended I spend the night. They hoped my vision would return within a few hours. I could not fly because of the pressurization, so I called a family member to drive me home the next day.

Thankfully, my eye healed in a few weeks, and I was able to fly again, but I dodged first class for a while; I wanted to stay away from those pesky champagne bottles!

Chapter 19

9-11

On September 10, 2001, I was about to leave on a three-day trip that started with a layover in Philadelphia. We left that morning on a non-stop flight to New Orleans on a 737-300, and I was the lead flight attendant. I usually did not mind being in charge, but on that particular day I wasn't feeling well. First class was full, as usual, and I had to serve breakfast choices of an egg omelet or French toast. Nothing odd happened during the flight, but as we made our descent, my ears began to pop, and I noticed a sharp pain in them. I had experienced ear infections several times before and I knew what was ahead: many hours of pain while flying.

When we got on the ground, the first officer asked us if we wanted a beignet, a pastry made famous in the city of New Orleans. They were first introduced by the French-Creole colonists in the eighteenth century. The recipe is simple: the dough is fried and then covered with mounds of sugar. We often purchased the treat in the New Orleans airport, a tradition I loved, although the snow-like white powder usually covered our navy-blue uniforms by the time we finished eating. Most of us felt the experience was worth the extra chore of brushing it off though.

Buying a King Cake was another much-loved tradition when we flew into New Orleans. King Cakes are usually made and eaten during the Carnival season. The round confections contain a feve—a small trinket—hidden inside. Folklore says that whoever gets the piece with the feve is awarded special privileges, so it was always fun to see who got the surprise. And it made for an excellent excuse to eat cake!

I finished my beignet and mentioned to the captain that my ears hurt and had especially bothered me during the landing. We talked for a few minutes, and he suggested I get off the trip.

"You can blow an eardrum that way," he explained.

I had damaged my ears years ago on a trip, so I knew he was right. I called scheduling and asked them to replace me in Charlotte. When I arrived home at 5:30 p.m., it was too late to go see my doctor, so I made plans to have my ears checked the next day.

I was in a deep sleep the morning of Tuesday, September 11, 2001. My sister, Cindy, called and woke me up a little after 9:00 a.m.

"Are you on a trip or are you home?" she asked urgently.

I felt startled to hear her asking such an odd question. "I got off my trip yesterday and I'm home now."

"Well, turn on the TV and see what's happened! One of your planes just flew into the World Trade Center."

"What in the world?" I immediately told her goodbye and turned on my bedroom TV. I felt like I was watching a movie, but sadly, it was reality. My thoughts turned to where I would have been that morning if I'd continued the trip I was on. Because of my ears, I was safely in my bed at home, watching events unfold from a distance. Many crews became stranded in different cities, unable to get home for days because of all airline service shutting down.

"At 8:46 a.m., five hijackers crashed American Airlines Flight 11 into the north façade of the World Trade Center's North Tower," said the reporter. "At 9:03 a.m., another five hijackers crashed United Airlines Flight 175 into the south façade of the South Tower."

I could hardly believe what I was hearing. My phone continued to ring most of the day. The two aircraft that were used as bombs on September 11 were not US Airways flights, nor were the other two planes involved, one of which hit the Pentagon and the other of which headed for Washington, D.C., but never reached its target because of the selfless acts of the passengers.

I later learned that some of the terrorists' plans had been curtailed because of the president's decision to stop air travel, an action that may have prevented additional hijackers from using our company's planes in another attack.

To say the least, it was an emotional day for everyone involved in the airline industry. Never in our country's history had we suffered such a massive loss of life so unexpectedly. Who would have ever suspected that terrorists would use airplanes as instruments of evil in such a vile act? But they had evidently found a glitch in our security systems that allowed them to carry out their well-planned assault.

All Americans knew that after that day, air travel would

never be the same. A week later, I flew again on my first trip after that disastrous day. I was assigned a flight to Los Angeles on the Airbus 321. Only forty-eight passengers joined us, so I moved as many people as I could up to first class. We gave out free drinks and meals because I felt that if they were willing to fly after what had happened, they deserved special treatment.

One couple that I moved to first class passed me an envelope as they left the aircraft. On the flight back to the east coast, I opened the envelope, and a hundred-dollar bill fell out. The enclosed note read:

"It takes a brave person to fly after what we witnessed on 9-11. We appreciate your making our flight both comfortable and special. We are on our way to see our son, who is in the military. He will be deployed soon; otherwise, we would not have flown today! Thank you for making our trip so nice."

It made me smile knowing that the small act of moving a few passengers to first class had made their flight better.

I had seen fear on people's faces as they boarded our flight that day, and it took a while for people to feel comfortable flying again. Our Flight Attendants' Union offered counseling for those crew members who experienced PTSD afterward. Many suffered from it because after we read the headlines and watched the news, it was always in the back of our minds that the same thing could have happened to us.

I cried a lot during those first weeks after September 11, 2001, mourning my fellow crew members and their families.

The airline industry felt the effects of that horrible day

more than most, and those events proved to be the beginning of the financial decline for US Airways that eventually drove the company to bankruptcy in 2002.

Three thousand lives were lost that day, and our world as we knew it would never be the same.

Chapter 20

TEETH

Darkness! I wish we had night vision goggles while working night flights!

West Coast and International trips were my favorites, so a lot of my flights happened in the dark. I preferred long-range flights for several reasons. Number one was because the boarding process was my least favorite of the airline procedures, and long-range flights had fewer of them. Second, I liked the opportunity of getting to know my passengers. When you have five or six flights a day, it leaves little time to do anything more than serve a drink and later pick it up. Some flights were so quick, we barely had time to serve; those are the ones where passengers may see us running to our jump seats before landing.

I was the "B" flight attendant on this trip on an Airbus 321. During a twenty-four-hour layover in Seattle, Washington, several of us decided to visit the local sights. We settled on a trip to Pike Place Market, where we planned to look around and then grab some fresh seafood. As we ventured there, I noticed that the air seemed especially crisp and clear. I had been to Seattle several times before, but it usually rained. We enjoyed our stop at the Fish Market, watching the merchants throw the fish back and forth to each other. (If you have never seen this, be sure to visit the Market on your next trip. It's quite a show!)

We left Seattle around 10:00 p.m. PST with a full flight. We had just finished our beverage service, so I called up front to tell Trena, the lead flight attendant, that it was time to turn the lights off in the cabin. She laughed and said that she had completed her service quickly and everyone was already asleep. The cabin went dark, and we took our seats in the back of the plane to read and talk until we landed in Charlotte. Occasionally we would take turns walking through the cabin to check on passengers and answer call bells.

I had learned early on in my career to take a nap at the hotel before a red-eye flight. The bell rang from Trena.

"Hey," she said, "I have ice cream left in first class if you want some." We accepted her offer, so I went to the front of the plane to bring it back with me. As I walked through the darkness in first class, I stumbled on something on the floor. After accidentally kicking it to the side, I got to the front and asked Trena for a napkin.

"Don't you want your ice cream first?" she asked.

"No, I need to see what I tripped over."

I used my small flashlight to search the right side of the aisle, and there it was—an upper set of dentures! I picked them up in the napkin and showed Trena.

"Who in the world has lost their teeth?" I asked her. We looked at each other and couldn't help but laugh. "We've got to find out who they belong to."

"You know they're going to be embarrassed when they find out their dentures were lying on the floor."

"Probably someone in an aisle seat," I said.

We discussed the situation and decided to use my flashlight to determine who'd lost their teeth. There were sixteen seats in first class and four rows of seats. All sixteen people were sound asleep. I started checking the aisle passengers in the first row, but as I was peering at a woman's mouth, she suddenly opened her eyes.

"I'm so sorry," I said, "but we're trying to find someone who's lost an item." She closed her eyes and seemed not to let the interruption bother her.

I checked rows two and three without success. Then I spotted an older man in 4D, and it was easy to see that his upper teeth were missing. Bingo! I hurried back to Trena and told her the mystery had been solved. She was still holding the teeth.

"What should we do now?" she asked.

"Well, you should probably do it without an audience around to spare him any embarrassment."

Since everyone else was asleep, we decided to wake the man and hope that nobody but us would ever know what the situation was. I walked up to him as quietly as I could, leaned down, and tapped him on the arm. He must have been in a deep sleep because it took several attempts to wake him. He finally looked up at me with a drowsy and questioning look, and I apologized for the disturbance.

"Sir, I think you dropped these in the aisle."

"Oh my heavens!" he gasped. When he spoke, he woke everyone around him, so they looked over to see what was happening.

"Why don't you come up front for a minute? You can visit the lavatory," I suggested. The lady beside him, most likely his wife, had been silent until now. She glanced at what was in the napkin and started fussing at him for always losing his teeth. I felt sorry for him, helped him out of his seat, and directed him to the bathroom. He remained in there for some time, long enough for everyone who was seated around him to fall back asleep. We flew for several more hours and then arrived in Charlotte.

Trena and I laughed later that maybe the passengers would all think it was a dream since they fell back to sleep so quickly. Sometimes reality and dreams are blurry in the middle of the night on a dark flight.

Chapter 21

DEAL

Most professions have their good and bad sides, and the job of flight attendant was no exception. For example, I dreaded October because I had to take yearly training and pass an exam as required by the company and the FAA. The two-day training was held in Charlotte, and I had to take it to continue flying. During the exam, we had to open and close all of the exits on each aircraft, review CPR and other medical procedures, and conduct evacuation drills. My husband always wondered why I got so nervous when it was time for the yearly training, but it was because I didn't conduct evacuations or do some of the other tasks very often. Still, remembering the verbiage and performing the procedures properly were important, so we flight attendants took it seriously. The training sure made for some frazzled nerves!

Most people think flight attendants are only onboard to attend to passenger comfort and serve drinks and food, but we do much more than that. We are trained to react to any emergency, medical or otherwise, that might happen on a flight, and luckily, only once in thirty-four years did I have to give CPR to a passenger.

On a Phoenix flight, in the middle of our dinner service, several call bells went off near seat 10D to alert us to a male passenger who appeared to be having a heart attack. He was unconscious, and I reached his seat first. When I realized we had a medical emergency onboard, I instructed another flight attendant to let the lead flight attendant know. The captain was then notified that we needed to land for a medical emergency. The other flight attendants and I moved the man as carefully as possible to the aisle, where we pumped his chest and gave him air until we landed. We always ask for medical assistance in a situation like that, and most flights usually have one or two doctors or nurses onboard, which is such a blessing. On this flight, a medic assisted us.

Thankfully, our training proved to be a valuable tool, and we later learned that the man recovered. That was one of many medical emergencies I encountered while flying. Some required onboard oxygen, and many involved panic attacks, which we'd been taught to recognize. Only once in thirty-four years did a passenger pass away while in the air. We tried desperately to revive him after he suffered a massive heart attack, but we were later told he did not survive.

Thankfully, most flights did not have medical emergencies, but we never knew when they might happen. We always needed to be prepared, never knowing if we'd be called on to assist in saving someone's life. I was often asked if I ever delivered a newborn in my years of flying. I must admit, I didn't have to use my baby-delivery skills, but

I'm sure it happens occasionally.

Game show contestants often flew on our flights to Los Angeles. On a 2008 flight to Los Angeles, I was working in the rear section of my favorite aircraft, the Airbus 321. We had 187 passengers, and since some of our jump seats faced the cabin, I could talk to passengers. I had just started a conversation with a sweet couple from Nashville who were accompanying their son and his family on the trip. Apparently, their son, Ben, was to be a contestant on the game show *Deal or No Deal*, taping the next morning at Culver City Studios. They said he was nervous, but they hoped—as everyone does—that he would win BIG!

As I was talking with them, the call bell went off in the back cabin. I immediately went to row 15, where the woman in the window seat said she was having trouble breathing. I asked the other passengers to move temporarily so I could sit next to her and evaluate her symptoms. After asking various questions, I determined that she was claustrophobic and feeling as if she were being smothered. I asked the passenger on the aisle if he would mind switching seats with her. He did, and we administered oxygen to the woman until she felt better. I saw this type of problem many times especially on long flights.

After we got her settled, I helped complete our onboard service. As I was putting the cart back in place, a young man approached me. "Would you mind holding my daughter while I go to the bathroom?" he asked.

I held my arms out to take his child. "Glad to help."

I later found out that his wife was in the other lavatory with their other child. When the man came out of the bathroom, he thanked me for watching his little girl. He returned to his seat, and I resumed picking up cups and cans. When I returned to the galley, the young man was walking with his daughter. He apologized for being in the way.

"You're fine!" I told him. "Lots of children get tired and restless on a long flight."

As we chatted, I realized that he was the son of the couple I had met, the one slated to be on *Deal or No Deal*. I told him I had a long layover in Culver City near the studio and that I would cheer him on from afar. As he departed the galley, he surprised and delighted me by asking if I would like to be in the audience of the show and sit with his family.

"Absolutely! I would love to."

He told me he would arrange a ticket for me and told me to arrive at the studio by noon PST. I didn't know how I would get there or what I would wear, but I couldn't wait to go.

I woke up at 9:00 a.m. the next morning. I needed to make some arrangements, and I needed to make them quickly in order to get to the studio on time. I checked to see what clothes I had brought with me. Unfortunately, I only had some shorts and a white T-shirt. I'd need something better than that to sit in the front row with his family.

I dressed without even taking the time to put on makeup, then walked across the street to the mall. I usually take my time when I go shopping, but I was on a mission! I remembered advice I'd read somewhere that said to avoid clothes with busy patterns if you are going to be on camera; apparently, they don't look good on television. I piled my shopping cart with six different outfits. I'm not very tall, so I was careful to pick capri pants that wouldn't require any hemming. Within thirty minutes, I purchased something cute and headed back to the hotel.

"What is the quickest and easiest way to get to the Culver City Studios?" I asked the bellman. He rattled off the local buses I could take and the multiple stops they would make, and I knew I would never get there in time. Since I needed to be at the show by noon, I asked him if he would be willing to take me in the hotel van. He must have felt sorry for me because he agreed to take me at 11:00 a.m., after dropping off a departing crew at the airport, which he did. Everything was falling into place, and I gave him a hefty tip for being so helpful.

I arrived at the studio at 11:30 a.m. and was excited to walk onto the set of a show I had watched many times. It was my mother's favorite game show, so I called her as I waited for Ben and his family to join me.

"Guess where I am?" I said.

"I have no idea."

"I'm sitting here looking at Howie Mandel!" I exclaimed. She was definitely surprised and told me that she would love to go one day. As a treat, I took her six months later.

The producer came over to my seat, introduced himself, and welcomed me. Before he walked away, he turned to me and whispered, "Just so you know, you won't be going up on the stage with the family if he wins."

He wanted to know how I knew the family and was surprised to learn that I had only met them the night before on my flight. Then Howie Mandel came by and gave us his

99

usual "fist knock." I found out later that he never shook hands because of his germophobia and OCD. He once wrote a comedy sketch called "Here's the Deal: Don't Touch Me." But he was very nice and started the show by welcoming everyone in the audience. Then he told us that this particular show would air during Thanksgiving week.

"Therefore," he said, "we are giving everyone in the audience a complimentary turkey."

I wondered how in the world I would get a big frozen turkey home on my flight, and I thought about that for the rest of the show.

As luck would have it, Ben won big that night. In fact, he won sixty-three thousand dollars, and his family joined him up on the stage. Being there was quite an experience, one I will never forget.

And about that turkey? Well, as I left the show, they handed us vouchers for a Butterball Turkey valued at up to twenty-five dollars. I rode the bus back to the hotel, which took three hours, so it was certainly a relief not to have to carry around a big frozen bird.

Flight crews see many unusual items brought onboard, but I've never seen anyone carrying a turkey!

Chapter 22

MIRACLE

It was January 15, 2009, a cold winter day in the airline industry. US Airways Flight 1549, an Airbus-320, and its Charlotte flight crew of six were on takeoff from La Guardia. As the aircraft gained altitude, a flock of Canadian geese struck the plane and caused it to lose all engine power. It's hard to imagine how it would feel to be onboard and suddenly hear a series of inexplicable, loud bangs, followed by the odor of fuel seeping in, and then silence.

As flight attendants, we become accustomed to the familiar sounds and sensations of the plane. We can sense when we're leveling off or making our descent, so an unusual silence on ascent would have alerted the crew and passengers to a problem. The flight attendants working Flight 1549 that day were Donna Dent, Sheila Dahl, and Doreen Walsh, and the captain's name—Chelsey B. "Sully" Sullenberger—has become familiar to all because of the way he handled a potentially disastrous situation.

Captain Sully was a former fighter pilot, a glider pilot, and an expert on aviation safety. Assisting him that day in the cockpit was First Officer Jeffrey B. Skiles, an experienced airline professional with over 20,500 career flight hours; however, this was First Officer Skiles's very first A-320 assignment since qualifying to fly it.

After power to the engines was lost, Captain Sully took over flying the plane. He and his copilot desperately tried to restart the engines, but they were unsuccessful. The aircraft continued to climb for another nineteen seconds until it reached 3,060 feet, and then it began a gliding descent. Captain Sully made a Mayday call to New York Control that they had encountered an emergency situation and were returning to La Guardia. They were directed to a runway, but the captain responded that he was "unable."

"We can't do it," he said in response to other landing options. "We're going to be in the Hudson."

Brace for impact! is the one command no one on a plane ever wants to hear. But that is exactly what was conveyed to the three flight attendants and one hundred fifty passengers who made an unpowered ditching into the middle of the North River section of the Hudson River that day. After the incident, the flight attendants would describe the ditch as a "hard landing" with "one impact, no bounce, and then a gradual deceleration."

After the landing, Captain Sullenberger opened the cockpit door.

"Evacuate!" he commanded. The flight attendants' years of training took over, and they got all of the passengers safely off of the sinking aircraft. As water filled the cabin, they told the people to climb over the seats. Ferries and rescue boats quickly arrived and took all the crew and passengers to land. The last person to leave the aircraft was the captain because he walked the length of the cabin to make sure no one had been left behind. He was a hero that day, but so was the rest of the crew!

I was sitting in the Charlotte crew room when I heard someone exclaim, "One of our planes crashed in the Hudson!"

Everyone rushed over to the television and watched in amazement. The fact that the flight crew was based in Charlotte made it especially personal. As I left on my own trip later, I reflected on all the possibilities, including, What would have happened if the plane had hit the George Washington Bridge? All kinds of questions passed through my mind, but I knew that God had performed a miracle, a miracle that needed just the right timing and circumstances. The plane hit the water at the perfect angle to keep the aircraft from breaking into pieces, and rescue boats had already been stationed nearby. Everyone involved had done an exemplary job that saved lives.

I later became friends with Sheila Dahl, one of the flight attendants on Flight 1549. I listened to her tell her story at a flight attendant meeting in Dallas. She said she wanted to take her one moment of fame and use it to help others, and she became instrumental in starting the Critical Incident Response Team (CIRT) for US Airways, a group of flight attendants from each base who assist fellow attendants who have experienced incidents or crises on or off the aircraft. The group is vital because only another flight attendant can understand the stress the job brings. I felt so privileged to serve on the CIRT with Sheila after she started it in 2011.

She once shared with me that she'd always kept a spiritual quote in her purse that gave her serenity: "Bidden or not bidden, God is present." That purse was destroyed on that fateful January day, but she later found a plaque with the same meaningful quote. After the incident, the words took on a whole new meaning for her because it became evident to her that God was truly present in every situation.

A movie was made of this spectacular event, and everyone who saw it agreed that it was truly a *MIRACLE ON THE HUDSON*!

Chapter 23

LAYOVERS

I cannot continue telling you about the life of a flight attendant without including some of my favorite layovers. As mentioned, we were in the habit of rating our layovers based on the quality of the restaurants, food, shopping, and sights in the area. We generally did not have transportation other than the hotel van, so it was a challenge to see a lot unless we rented a car or took a cab.

When in the states, we did not have to contend with the problem of a language barrier. We could ask anyone on the street about area attractions and then get directions. I also used a paper map to get around until I finally got a cell phone with Google Maps on it. After a few visits to a particular city, I could find my way around easily, so I began to compile a list of my favorite destinations.

San Diego, California, is one of my favorites for sure. The weather is consistently sunny, and the temperatures are in the seventies all year round, with little to no humidity. I remember one layover there with my friend Mary. We rented bikes and took the ferry to Del Coronado Island. We had heard it was beautiful, and we also wanted to see the Coronado Hotel, where *Some Like It Hot,* starring Marilyn Monroe, was filmed. It was spectacular to see the grand pink hotel up close as we cruised by on our bikes. We rode all day and stopped only for lunch and an ice cream afterward. In my home state of Virginia, most of the bike trails are challenging, so it was a real treat to enjoy a full day of biking without even breaking a sweat.

New York City is another favorite place to visit. It took me a few times before I felt comfortable traveling on the subway, but with time, I realized it wasn't as bad as the movies sometimes made it out to be. One bad experience, though, did teach me to always keep an eye on my surroundings because you never know who's lurking in the shadows, ready to prey on unsuspecting victims. As I waited for the train one day, a woman grabbed my Coach purse off my shoulder, but I gave chase and snagged it back. I grabbed the strap that was dangling beside her and won the battle. She turned around and spat at me, then said something I would rather not repeat. There wasn't much money in the bag, but it had been a gift and I sure didn't want to lose it. Before that incident, I didn't know I could run so fast!

Another valuable lesson I learned through the years is not to walk around while on a cell phone. Your focus is not on the crowd around you, and you can easily become a victim.

I always enjoyed seeing Broadway shows, going shopping, and taking city tours. One of my favorite tours was the Circle Line around the Statue of Liberty by boat. At night, the lights of the Big Apple are spectacular.

My favorite place in the world is Carmel, California. I was fortunate to know someone there, and I visited many times. I enjoyed the art, walking on the beach, and the quaint shops. Carmel has it all, including beautiful sunsets and cottages with thatched roofs that would entice most anyone. And the famous Pebble Beach Golf Course is within a few miles. It's known as one of the most beautiful courses in the world, and I was privileged to play there once. I'm not much of a golfer, but it was fun to make good memories.

Many of the hotels where we stayed during international layovers were close to train stations, and the crew usually planned to tour or eat out together during our time away. One of my favorite places to go overseas in Europe was Venice. I flew there once while based in Philadelphia. The rest of the crew had already flown that trip many times, but the one time I got to go, it was pouring rain. I was not in the habit of venturing out by myself in other countries, but I was determined to see the highlights of Venice, so I asked the hotel concierge the best way to tour the city. We were on the outskirts of town, so he told me to take a bus or taxi to get there. I went to my room, hurriedly got dressed, then went to the local bus stop two blocks away. I couldn't speak Italian, but I still managed to find my way, pay the fare, and get off at the correct stop. After I did, the rain stopped, and it turned into a gorgeous day for sightseeing.

There before me was the beautiful city of Venice, sometimes called the City of Canals. I stood for a few minutes and took in my surroundings. I strolled over one of the many bridges and spotted a gondola floating on the water below. A typical gondola ride costs eighty euros, or approximately ninety dollars, so I decided that while I would love to take a ride by myself on the canal, I would save that romantic treat for a possible future trip with my husband. I visited several small shops and bought some Murano glass jewelry, then I watched adults and children alike pass by as I dined at an outdoor café. It seemed that walking was the primary way people got around in spite of how easy it was to get lost. The many street intersections formed a complicated and confusing maze, at least for a tourist like me, but eventually they all ended up on the Grand Canal. I stayed alert and aware of my surroundings, and after six hours, I even managed to find my bus stop again. I slept on the thirty-minute ride back to the hotel, then headed to my room to sleep some more. I slumbered like a baby until the next morning when we all departed for the airport. The time in Venice was well worth it, even though I'd stayed up for over twenty-four hours the previous day.

Another lovely layover was Madrid, where I flew a few months later. We stayed in a downtown hotel, and as we checked in, the agent at the front desk reminded us that it was not safe to walk around by ourselves after dark. A few of my coworkers and I met in the lobby in the afternoon and went to the local grocery stores, where we bought local specialties, such as stuffed olives and delicious cheeses.

In Europe, it's customary to eat dinner around 9:00 p.m. or even later. But as it got close to dinnertime, I realized I had sampled too many delicacies already, and I had no appetite. In fact, my stomach felt rather queasy. I told the others I would skip dinner and walk back to the hotel, even though darkness was fast approaching. I was sure I could find my way back since there was an hour of daylight left.

As I strolled, I noticed all of the construction on the street. Beautiful buildings surrounded me, and several art exhibits caught my eye. I was certain I was headed in the right direction as some of the places looked familiar, but when I reached an intersection, I was unsure which way to go. Right? Left? Straight? As I grew more confused, I looked around for a nice passerby to help me. I asked three people for help, but each of them said, "No English." The sky turned dark, and I was getting anxious, so I did what I always do when I become afraid or need help: I began to pray.

"Dear Lord," I pleaded, "please help me know which way to go."

I had just finished my simple prayer when a loud male voice called out. "Sharon! Over here!" I looked up at the sky, thinking that God had chosen that moment to shout at me. I had never heard a loud verbal answer from above, but who else could it have been?

He called to me again, and I realized the voice was coming from a man seated in a café across the street. It was one of the pilots on my flight. He must have seen me on the corner, looking utterly lost. What a relief, and what an answer to prayer! I was sure it was not a coincidence that he had been sitting at that very spot and noticed me among the many in that big city. God had once again protected me, as He had many times before.

One of most memorable transatlantic layovers was in July 2014. Five of my peers from the 1984 Flight Attendant Class and I decided to fly a fun trip to celebrate our thirtieth anniversary. We flew to London and enjoyed a "sisterhood" reunion. How amazing to once again see and fly with these longtime friends. We reminisced about our early days of learning and counted how many fellow classmates were still flying after thirty years. Sadly, only twelve of forty-six flight attendants still remained on the seniority list. Many had left early in their careers when bases closed, having elected not to move or commute. Others had chosen different paths.

We had a wonderful time touring around, taking the train to the Tower of London, seeing the royal jewels, shopping at various boutiques, and dining at a local pub. Layovers like this could certainly renew one's excitement for continuing this longtime career.

Italy, Paris, Rome, Dublin, and Frankfurt were my other favorite international layovers. Each place had its own charms, and whenever I walked their streets, I reflected on their amazing histories. I stood and watched artists painting on the streets of Paris. I asked local people about their history in Dublin. I tasted many local foods, including sauerbraten and spaetzle in Frankfurt, pastries in Paris, and local pasta in Rome. And in Italy, of course, I could never resist buying cold, sweet Gelato because there was no better way to cool down on a hot afternoon.

Regardless of the beauty I encountered while traveling, I was always happy to return to the United States and hear the sweet words, "Welcome back home."

A favorite quote by Lin Yutang sums up my feelings when I return home: "No one realizes how beautiful it is to travel until he comes home and rests his head on his old, familiar pillow."

Chapter 24

BLESSINGS

I could not finish my book without dedicating a chapter to the many ways God blessed me with passengers and crew interactions.

Often, I flew with crewmembers who were fellow Christians. On the jump seat, we usually shared stories about our faith and how it affected our lives. Several times over the years, I left to go on trips while upset over events in my personal life. It was not by accident that on those occasions, there was usually a fellow flight attendant who provided encouragement.

One such trip occurred during my divorce. I cried most of the way to the airport only to find that I could not get a flight to Charlotte. Another flight attendant, Carole, was also trying to get there, so I invited her to ride with me. We didn't know each other well, but after a short time in the car, I began sharing my heartbreak. She shared scripture and encouraged me with sound advice, and by the time we arrived at our base, I felt much better. The pain still lingered, but it had helped to vent my frustrations to someone who truly listened. Sometimes all we need to do for others is be available to listen when they are going through a rough time. It was not by accident that Carole and I were at the ticket counter together, both trying to get to Charlotte.

Months later, on a flight to Chicago, I was working in first class and noticed an attractive middle-aged woman. She had a sad look on her face as she smiled and said hello, but her smile didn't reach her eyes. After she took her seat in 2A, I offered her something to drink while we were still on the ground, but she said she didn't care for anything. I noticed her box of tissues on her armrest but stayed quiet about it.

After takeoff, I turned on the oven for meal preparation, then checked on the passengers. When I reached the woman's seat, I noticed she was turned toward the window, crying. I asked if she wanted a meal and something to drink, but she said she didn't want anything other than a glass of water. I completed my service in an hour and decided to check the back cabin and help with their service. As I passed by 2A, I noticed the woman was bent and still crying—and it was not by accident that the seat beside her was empty. I stopped and sat down in 2C, then reached over and asked if I could get her anything.

"Can you mend a broken heart?" she asked.

Perhaps she was hurting in a way I could not help her, but on second thought, maybe I could. I asked if she wanted to talk about it, and then she turned to me and poured her heart out. Her husband had left the round-trip ticket for this flight on their kitchen table the night before, when he left her. She had gone to a prayer meeting, and he took that opportunity to clean out his closet and leave a note saying the marriage was over and that he was in love with another woman. He was "nice enough" to leave the ticket to Chicago so the woman could visit their daughter. Ironically, after leaving her, he'd figured she would not want to be alone.

As she ended her story, I hugged her and said I might have something that would help. She gazed at me through tears and said she knew God would help her through this, but it just hurt so badly. I went to the front galley, reached into my tote bag, and retrieved my Bible and the handout from my own Bible study the night before. The topic for the study? Divorce Care.

The handout detailed scriptures to read when you're hurt, sad, or depressed. It had been a comfort to me to read, and I hoped it would be the same for her. After I handed them to her, she thanked me and explained that she'd left so hurriedly that she hadn't packed anything to read. "Even my Bible is in my checked suitcase," she said.

I smiled and told her to let me know if she needed anything else. With an hour left on the flight, I checked on her. She was still reading. Later, after most everyone had deplaned, she was still in her seat. As I approached, she stood and handed me back my Bible and papers.

"You were my angel today," she said. "The scriptures were such a comfort. They've lifted my spirits, and I know there is hope now."

I told her to keep the paper with the scriptures and that I would be praying for her.

As I watched her walk out the forward door onto the jetway, a sense of thankfulness overtook me. God had given me an opportunity to share my faith just as Carole had shared hers with me months prior. I had been hurting from a divorce too, and someone had been there; someone had been my angel. God is so good. As a believer, I look for opportunities to share my faith. I try to be aware of people around me who are hurting and might need a listening ear. Though there may be times we all may feel we would not make a difference, God may nudge us and tell us differently.

I still remember a Miami–Charlotte flight from December 2012. I left that morning for the four-day trip with a real burden, and I was not feeling myself. I had met with an obstetric oncologist the week prior and found out that I needed surgery to determine if I had ovarian cancer. Thoughts of cancer changing my life kept swirling around in my head.

The heavy aircraft took off and I was soon working the first-class cabin. In row 4, two men were discussing their recent mission trip. I usually don't eavesdrop on conversations, but I did overhear some details. I asked a few questions about their trip and eventually discovered I was talking to Billy Graham's grandson. I told him what his grandad and dad's ministry meant to me, and when I returned to retrieve his meal trays, he asked me where I was from. Without thinking, I leaned down and asked if he would pray for me.

"What can I pray for you about?" he asked.

I teared up and told him I was having surgery the next week to find out if I had ovarian cancer.

He looked at me in dismay. "Why don't I pray for you right now?"

"Right now in first class?" I said.

"No time like the present."

I leaned down, and he took my hand and prayed for me on the spot. A sense of calmness came over me as I listened to his prayer. Never in thirty years had anyone done this for me in the middle of first class.

I suddenly felt a hand on my back. As the powerful prayer ended, I turned to see who had placed their hand on my back. It was the woman from the seat across the aisle. She said she felt compelled to join in our prayer and asked how she could help.

God supplied my needs that day in sending not one but two people to pray—strangers I'd never even met. God was showing me through them that He loved and would take care of me. The following week when I had my surgery, I felt that no matter the outcome, I would be okay. I got a call on Christmas Eve that I did not have cancer. That was one of the best Christmas gifts I ever received.

Part IV

AMERICAN AIRLINES

"If I rise on the wings of the dawn,
if I settle on the far side of the sea,
even there your hand will guide me."

~ Psalm 139

Chapter 25

WIG

In 2012, we once again heard rumors of a merger, and by 2013, it was announced that US Airways and American Airlines would combine to create the largest airline in the world. It amazed me that Piedmont, once a small regional airline, became part of a huge corporation.

Buzz filled the crew room as we speculated about exciting changes that might be made, but at the same time, we dreaded the classes we would need to take to integrate the two systems after the merger.

What will our new uniforms look like? Will they close our base again? Will there be layoffs? These were just a few of the questions in the days after the news broke.

I've already said that I preferred west coast trips. On one trip, I was the lead flight attendant on an Airbus 321, and we were all looking forward to a long layover in Las Vegas. After the plane took off, I busied myself getting drink and meal orders for the first-class passengers. With sixteen first-class seats, it was quite a task to get all the meals and drinks out in a timely manner.

Once the lights were dimmed, most of the passengers went quiet. I took the opportunity to sit down and read one of my favorite Mary Higgins Clark books. (By the way, Ms. Clark served as a flight attendant before turning to a career in writing.) I had been on my feet for almost three hours, and I needed a break. Just as I settled in, a call bell rang. I got up and approached a seemingly pleasant, elderly man seated in 3F.

"I need new headphones," he yelled at me. "These aren't working."

At that time, we gave out larger headphones than we do now so that passengers could watch the in-flight movie after dinner.

I asked him to hand them to me and told him I would get him a new pair. When I returned, he thanked me and placed them on his head. I was then free to return to my novel, but as I sat down, the call bell rang again.

Up I went. Same man.

"I still can't hear anything," he complained.

"Have you tried turning the volume up on the dial inside your armrest?"

"I didn't know anything about that!"

I leaned over him and adjusted the volume. "Can you hear anything now?"

"No. Still can't hear anything!"

"Let me have them, and I'll check them out."

"What?" he shouted, the elevated sound of his voice clearly agitating the woman next to him. But who could blame her? The man obviously couldn't hear, with or without the headphones, so I reached over and lifted them off of his head. But when I looked down to inspect them, I noticed I was also holding his hairpiece in my hand.

"Hey!" he shouted. "You took my hair!"

The situation caused the lady on the aisle to laugh loudly. I didn't know what to do, so I placed the toupee back on the man's bald scalp. But rather than help the situation, it caused the other passengers to put on their overhead lights to see what was going on. I worked very hard to refrain from laughing myself.

I returned my gaze to the man. His lopsided hairpiece tilted to the left, but at least it was back where it belonged. With that settled, I went to the galley and determined that the headphones were working properly. Perhaps his seat connection was malfunctioning, but there were no empty seats to move him to.

I took a deep breath to compose myself, then returned to the man's seat, all the time wishing I could summon a mechanic to help me.

"Sir," I said, "I am so sorry, but these headphones seem to be working. It must be the connector in your armrest that's not functioning."

The lady beside him offered to trade seats. "I really don't want to watch the movie, anyway," she said. "I'd rather sleep."

Thank goodness for nice folks on the plane! Her offer seemed to satisfy him.

With his hairpiece still crooked, and one side of it hanging over his left ear, he stood up to change seats, but I whispered to him to follow me to the galley first. Once there, I suggested he pop into the lavatory to fix his hair. I again apologized, and to my relief, he laughed.

"Wait until I tell my friends back home that a flight

attendant messed up my hair in the dark!" he said with a wink.

After fixing his appearance, he returned to his seat and watched the movie, this time with sound. But fifteen minutes later, as I passed by, I saw that he was fast asleep. I stood there and thought about all the trouble we had just gone through so he could hear the movie.

When we landed in Las Vegas, I shared this story with the other flight attendants. "We really should write a book about these crazy airplane stories!" I added.

I started keeping a journal the next week.

Chapter 26

CHANGES

Any merger represents a scary and anxious time for employees. We had already been through one major merger when Piedmont was bought by USAir, and while we went through a lot of changes then, it was nothing compared to the merger with American Airlines.

Within that year, the familiar changed. We had numerous online classes to "relearn" our jobs. The more senior flight attendants would often comment that "it's hard to teach old dogs new tricks!" I hate to admit it, but I was one of those old dogs, and I found the learning process more challenging than I had when I was younger.

We got new uniforms, but many of the flight attendants developed allergic reactions to them. The union sent the clothing off to be tested, and they reportedly found a few inconsequential problems, but because the company received so many complaints of health problems, they replaced the uniforms by 2020.

We added more bases, and our corporate headquarters moved to the Dallas–Fort Worth area. Doug Parker, the

CEO of US Airways became the CEO of what is now known as American Airlines. The merger meant US Airways ceased to exist, which caused a certain degree of sadness in that the company we had all worked for was gone. My memories of the fun times on the planes and during layovers remain among my most cherished. US Airways was the company that provided me a steady income and job security, enabling me to live well even in the bleakest times after 9-11.

On the upside, we had become a part of the largest airline in the world! *Who would have thought little old Piedmont Airlines would become part of that?*

We former US Airways employees remained on our separate airplanes and routes until 2015, when the airlines finally merged their services. Crews were then transferred to other bases. We began to see new faces in Charlotte, and the flight attendants that had been commuting from the west coast were able to transfer back to Los Angeles and San Francisco.

Under US Airways, everything within the employee guidelines centered around seniority. Seniority determined the trips you were awarded to fly, what position you flew during a trip, and if you could get on a flight to get to work. One of the downsides of the merger was that we lost our seniority in employee travel. It became a contest to see who could sign in first to travel on certain flights. First sign-in got on first within the twenty-four-hour period before the departure of a flight. This made it especially hard to commute.

Thank goodness that Charlotte, North Carolina, was kept as a hub, enabling me to remain based there. We expanded some of our international destinations after the merger, so I began flying to more European destinations.

One of the new cities added from Charlotte was Rome. I still remember walking to Trevi Fountain, ascending the Spanish Stairs, and eventually taking the train to various parts of the city. On one particular night, I was returning to the hotel after dinner with my fellow flight attendants, and we heard the most beautiful music coming from somewhere in the distance. Eventually, we came across an orchestra playing on an outdoor terrace that overlooked the Colosseum. It was breathtaking! We listened to that music well into the night while viewing the lights of the ancient buildings all around us. That is a memory I will never forget.

Chapter 27

BEACH

In 2015, we were still adjusting to our schedules after the transition to American Airlines, and changes continued to be made within the work groups. I stayed busy flying mostly international trips but also mixed it up with US cities that I enjoyed. I was then in my thirty-first year of flying. Wow! Amazing how time passed by so quickly.

One Saturday morning, I was packing to go on a three-day trip to Los Angeles, where I planned to spend time on the beach. I didn't usually fly on the weekends anymore, but it was the end of the month and I still needed fifteen hours to fulfill my flying obligations, so I picked up this sweet trip. We arrived in Los Angeles around 8:00 p.m. PST, and after I checked into the hotel, I reserved a bike so I could get to the beach the following day. It was only a mile away.

I got up early the next day and breakfasted at the Pancake House. Afterward, I got on my somewhat dilapidated bike, with a towel and my Bible in the front basket. I wanted some quiet time and couldn't think of a better place to have it than at the beach. As I cycled along the sidewalk, an older couple walked toward me. Since I didn't possess the best riding skills, I steered off the sidewalk to let them pass. Big mistake! I hit a pothole, which caused the pedal of the old bike to fall off! Then I crashed right in front of the couple and, with a lot of noise, fell to the pavement. The man and woman ran over to see if I was okay. I grinned and told them that only my pride had been injured.

Given that I hadn't ridden a bike in ten years, I shouldn't have been surprised to be wobbly on two wheels. But, undeterred, I dropped the pedal into the basket and got right back on the rickety contraption. It didn't make for an ideal cycling situation, but the sun was shining, and the beach was calling my name, so off I went. In a few minutes, I reached the edge of the Pacific Ocean. Such a beautiful sight. Then, hearing some people talking to my left, I turned and noticed a group gathered on the beach with lounge chairs. Being the nosy person that I am, I approached a woman standing near the group.

"What kind of gathering is this?" I asked.

"It's Cornerstone Church," she said. "We hold our services near the water, and today we're having testimonies and baptisms." She smiled. "Why don't you join us?"

Before I even answered, she told her husband to run across the street and fetch another chair.

"Well," I said, "I guess I'll be staying."

As I listened to the young pastor talk about their ministry and the many people who had made decisions for Christ that summer, I looked past him and saw a man painting a seascape on a huge canvas. I wondered why the artist was painting during the service and not joining the rest of us.

After the new believers had offered their testimonies, I was invited to walk with everyone to the water to see the baptisms. I had never seen or experienced anything like this before, and it was amazing to hear the baptism aspirants share stories of their dismal pasts and hopes for new futures. To witness them being baptized, not in a church but in the ocean, where we could all see them, is something I will never forget.

One of my hobbies is painting. I have dabbled in oils and acrylics over the years, and I've always planned to teach art upon retirement. I even took my watercolors with me on quite a few trips. Out of curiosity, I approached the seascape artist and watched him make talented strokes on the canvas.

"Is there a reason you paint during the church service?" I asked.

"The first reason to do a painting," he said, turning to me, "is to sell it and use the money to support our beach ministry. The second reason is to have my own sermon." He gazed at me with sincerity in his eyes. "Our life is like an empty canvas until God fills it with beauty."

I nodded in agreement, knowing his statement was true. Then I trekked up the beach, retrieved my chair, and returned it with my gratitude to the people who had made me feel so welcome. Afterward, I rode my bike on the beach trail for a few hours before heading back to the hotel.

The blessing I received from that trip was that despite working the flight out of necessity to fulfill my hours, it turned out to be one of my favorite layovers ever. If I had not chosen to ride a bike to the beach, God wouldn't have been able to surprise me that day. It's those unexpected blessings in life that we need to treasure.

Chapter 28

OOPS!

On a flight to Boston, Massachusetts, several years ago, we were an hour from landing when a call bell rang. I went to the passenger in seat 12D and asked how I could help him.

"Something's dripping on my head," he said. "It's coming out of the overhead compartment."

As he spoke, I noticed wet spots on his jacket and in his hair. The liquid appeared to be milky in texture. I opened the overhead bin to see if something might have spilled, but I didn't see an overturned bag or any evidence of a problem.

"Hmm," I said, "I don't see where the leak is coming from." The drip continued, so I placed a few tissues in the seam of the overhead. "I'll be right back."

I returned to the back galley to confer with the other flight attendants, but it suddenly dawned on me that perhaps the liquid was coming from the bin *in front* of his seat. During takeoff, something might have tilted back, thus causing the leak. I returned to 12D, where the tissues clearly weren't working. I opened the bin over row 11 and BINGO, there was an overturned cooler with liquid surrounding it.

"Who does this belong to?" I asked the nearby passengers. A young mom holding a baby raised her hand and said it was her breast milk.

Before I had a chance to tell the man, he jumped up with a look of disgust. "Are you telling me I have her breast milk dripping all over me?"

The woman seemed shocked at his reaction and reassured him she didn't know the cooler was leaking. I asked him to follow me to the galley, where I handed him a can of club soda, aka Flight Attendant's Spot Remover.

"Sir, you can go in the bathroom and clean it off of your jacket and hair."

"Does milk stain?" he asked.

"I don't think so. But even if it does, you're sure going to have a funny story to tell."

He laughed as he closed the door.

Several weeks later, on a flight to Newark, New Jersey, I was getting drink orders and meal requests from the passengers in first class when I noticed an especially nice-looking gentleman in 1C. He wore a tailored suit and a spotless, starched white shirt. After taking orders, I made the drinks and prepared the meals. I was ready to serve Mr. Starch Shirt his chicken and Diet Coke on a tray, but as I entered the aisle, a young woman ran right into me and bumped the tray. The Diet Coke turned over, spraying everyone like a fire hose. Would you like to guess who got sprayed the most?

The man in the now-wet tailored suit jumped up. "I'm soaked!"

If I could have crawled into a hole, I would have. "I'm so sorry," I told him, knowing that wouldn't really help the situation. I quickly got him some trusty club soda and hot towels.

"What am I supposed to do with these?" he asked.

He was really upset, so I opened the lavatory door and gestured for him to enter. He hesitated but eventually disappeared inside without another word. I went to help the other passengers, although they didn't seem quite as upset.

The man stayed in the bathroom for a while, and when he came out, he seemed in a better mood. I offered him a cleaning voucher, which he accepted with a smile. And the next time I served first class, I remembered to move very slowly around the corner. No more accidents, please!

Chapter 29

MISSING

In 2017, my friend Mary and I flew a trip together to Los Angeles so we could go to the *Dr. Phil Show*. I had been in the audience several times on layovers and was always impressed with Dr. Phil's knowledge and advice. We enjoyed a taping of two shows and got back to the hotel in plenty of time to rest before flying back overnight.

Working with the public all of my adult life, it's become somewhat of a hobby of mine to study people's habits and body language. Plus, I did a college term paper about body language, so I know there is much information to be gleaned by studying human behavior. It was beneficial to me when dealing with passengers, and I found I could read most people and their intentions fairly quickly. But sometimes even I got stumped.

On the post-Dr. Phil, red-eye flight back to Charlotte, I was collecting cups when a man in the center seat in row 26 stopped me.

"I don't mean to bother you," he said, "but the man who was next to me has disappeared." He seemed genuinely concerned as he pointed to the aisle seat beside him.

"How long has he been missing?" I asked.

The man kept his eyes on the empty seat. "Probably an hour."

"What did he look like?"

"Tall with dark hair."

He'd just described most of the men on our flight. "Did he behave strangely in any way?" I asked.

He shrugged. "Not any stranger than most people."

"One thing is for certain," I said with a wink before walking away, "he's somewhere on this airplane."

I returned to the back galley and told Mary that we seemed to have a missing person onboard. We checked the passenger list and found his name but didn't announce it because it was late, and most people were sleeping.

"Well," Mary said, "let's start the hunt."

We laughed at the idea of looking for him under the seats and in the overhead bins because as we tried to stay awake all night, giddy humor sometimes took over! We searched the cabin and the seats that were supposed to be empty; when the lights go down, passengers often move around the cabin. But the missing man wasn't in any of the unassigned seats.

Then, in the back galley, I noticed that the line to both lavatories was really long. Six people were waiting, which was unusual so late at night. One lady even grabbed my arm as I passed and asked if there were other lavatories. I told her she could use the one in first class and directed her to it.

"Someone must be sick in one of the bathrooms," she said, "because they've been in there forever."

I looked at Mary and smiled. "Our mystery man."

I could tell by her expression that she was thinking the same thing. I knocked on the lavatory door. "Are you okay?" I asked.

"I'm fine," said a male voice from inside.

"Sir, we've been looking for you." I stayed near the door to better hear him.

"I'm doing fine in here. Don't worry about me."

"There are other people waiting to use the bathroom. Can you please come out and go to your seat?"

Several moments passed before I heard another response.

"Just leave me alone. I'm okay and want to stay in here!"

Several of the people in line stared at the door agape.

"Sir, I don't want to have to tell you again, but you need to come out NOW!"

"Why?" he said in an irritated voice.

A moment later, the door cracked open. I didn't know what to expect when the door fully opened, but I hoped it wouldn't be anything obscene. It wasn't. What I saw was a middle-aged man sitting on the toilet, fully clothed in a business suit, with a newspaper in his hands.

"I would rather sit here and read," he said. "I'm not coming out."

He went to close the door again, but I grabbed it.

"It isn't safe for you to be in there for an extended period of time," I said, grasping for ways to make him exit, "and there's no seatbelt in there." I guess my reasons resonated with him because he grunted a few times, stood, then exited the small enclosure and squeezed by the other passengers. By that time, we had an audience of at least eight. As he passed them, they started clapping, but he waved their loud ovation away and sat down. He did not seem happy.

Mary and I later discussed the man's unusual behavior.

"I wonder what Dr. Phil would say to him," Mary said.

"Evidently, the security of that small bathroom was his happy place," I said. "Though I guess we'll never know for sure."

Chapter 30

ANIMALS

In mid-2014, a young woman boarded a Connecticut-to-D.C. US Airways flight with a seventy-pound pot-bellied pig. The robust and evidently strong twenty-something carried Porky over her shoulder and brought it onboard as an emotional support animal. The passenger beside the woman reported that she tethered the animal's leash to the armrest and then allowed it to walk up and down the aisle, followed by a stink that could be smelled throughout the cabin.

Since 2012, emotional support animals have been allowed on flights per federal rules, but it is at the discretion of the crew as to whether or not the pet behaves well enough to fly. In the aforementioned case, a pig should not fly! While I was not on the flight with the excited pot-bellied pet, it did make national news. Other unusual pets that boarded planes included ducks, rabbits, birds, horses, monkeys, and kangaroos.

A parrot boarded one of my flights in 2013. The colorful bird was perched on the shoulder of a man who handed me his Emotional Support Animal certificate, which had been signed by his physician. I helped him to his aisle seat and talked to him about his pet. He assured me that he had flown many times with his feathered friend and that the bird always behaved well.

"Do you have a cage to put the bird in before we take off?" I asked.

"No, he'll sit right here with me the whole flight."

We were flying on an Airbus 321, and my jump seat was located behind him, though I had my back to him. When we lifted off the runway for takeoff, I heard a commotion in the cabin. I whipped around, horrified to see the parrot flying over passengers' heads and squawking in distress. This, of course, got everyone's attention, and many were laughing as the man chased the bird around. I cringed and hoped this wouldn't turn into a scene from Alfred Hitchcock's *The Birds*.

"Everyone, please remain in your seats until the seat belt sign is turned off," I announced as the man ran around shouting in both Spanish and English.

"Pedro!" he yelled, his arms flailing helplessly after the parrot. "Pedro! *Ven aca*, Pedro! Come here!"

A minute later, Pedro alit on his owner's shoulder. Once we leveled off, I got up to check the cabin. Several passengers asked if they could have a towel to clean up the bird droppings on their clothes. Evidently, Pedro had caused quite a mess in his short span of time on the loose.

On a recent flight, I had to deal with seventeen assistance animals, definitely a record for me. There were six cats and eleven dogs, and as the number of animals onboard increased, so did my allergic reactions.

At one point, while conducting the beverage and meal service, I began sneezing and could not stop because there were three cats in the two rows beside me. Trying to serve drinks while sniffling and sneezing doesn't make a good mix. I had to leave the cart and ask the other flight attendant to switch places with me because I have been allergic to cats since childhood.

As all the pets left the aircraft with their owners, one elderly couple waited patiently in their seats, so I asked them if I could help them deplane. They both commented on all the cats and dogs in the cabin, and I smiled. "Yes, they seem to be getting more popular."

I helped them out of their seats and noticed the man's pants were sliding down. It's always a difficult moment when I have to tell someone that something embarrassing is about to happen, so I whispered to him that he might want to pull his pants up. He looked at me, but I wasn't sure he had heard me, and as I followed them both with their bags, I had to helplessly watch his pants slowly fall to his ankles. He didn't seem to notice and continued walking until his wife turned around to speak to him.

"Henry!" she screamed. "Where are your pants?" He looked down and saw where they were. "I told you to wear a belt today!" the wife continued.

After they left the aircraft, I could still hear her fussing at him because apparently, after he'd pulled up his pants, they slowly fell down again.

Whether it was dealing with flying parrots or falling pants, nothing really surprised us in our profession—even when both events happened on the same flight!

In January 2020, a proposal was made by the

Department of Transportation to overhaul the regulations regarding service animals. A new rule was then put in place that allowed passengers to bring only dogs with them and to restrict those passengers who falsely claimed their pets were service animals. People who legitimately need a support dog now have to fill out a federal form that attests to the fact that the animal has been specifically trained to help them. This should limit the number of animals on planes and help both the crews and the flying public.

Chapter 31

TODAY

After I broke my left femur on February 26, 2018, while chasing that cute little dog, I underwent emergency surgery. Even though I now have a rod and several screws in my thigh, my leg feels normal most of the time. I was sixty-two years old at the time of my accident, and the doctor told me that I would likely always have pain. Later, I learned that my bone had broken so easily because I'd been taking a medication to prevent and reverse bone loss. Ironically, because it had been prescribed long-term, it had essentially turned my bones into chalk. My fractured femur had been a disaster-in-waiting for years, so I gave thanks that the bone had held out as long as it did.

Since the job of a flight attendant requires lots of standing and moving about, I couldn't work during the six months it took me to walk unaided. During that time, I reflected on what my life would be like without the job I loved. I had been employed since the age of fifteen, when I worked as a waitress during high school. Over the course of those hundred and eighty days on disability, I felt a void in my life and spent much time in prayer over the issue. I also had to work hard to be disciplined and not resume my activities too fast.

Eventually, I made the decision to give my notice of retirement from American Airlines in October 2018. It was a bittersweet choice because it meant I would not be able to fly a "last flight"—the one we flight attendants always looked forward to flying. And it meant I'd never get to say goodbye to the many friends I had flown and worked with. Officially, the last time I served as a flight attendant was a February 2018 flight to San Francisco, which turned out to be fitting because that destination had always been my favorite.

Changes are forever being made in the industry, and airline life has certainly continued without me, but writing this book has helped me find closure. I experienced a profound sense of absence and loss when forced to leave behind my beloved occupation, as I'm sure many others have when leaving their chosen professions. It was therefore fun to reminisce through the years and remember the events that made up my unusual career path.

I am still able to fly for free and have enjoyed several nice trips since retirement. Amanda and I flew to Aruba last December and relished every minute of our mother-daughter trip. While flying, she laughed at how many times I reached up and closed the overhead bins. I told her it would take a while to deactivate the habits I had acquired during my time as a flight attendant. After all, it had been my life for many years. Another nice aspect of our life has been making a dream come true by purchasing a condo at the beach. My husband and I are able to fly to Myrtle Beach for long weekends and vacations there whenever possible. I call the beach "my happy place," and I look forward to many more days there.

As for my life in Virginia, I am involved in volunteer work and have begun teaching those art lessons, which I wholly enjoy. I'm painting more than ever, and I've been able to spend more time with my husband and family.

Last year, I shared with a flight attendant friend that since I retired, my dreams are often filled with the anxieties of travel. She said she had similar dreams after she quit flying, so perhaps it is normal. Luckily, those nightmares have since faded away. Maybe it just took a while for my brain to shut off the subconscious thoughts of a life that revolved around constant travel and schedules. I once estimated that I flew 2,450,000 miles in my career. That is a lot of miles in a lifetime!

I'm so thankful for my experiences so far. Flying has given me confidence and joy, and I've learned that people throughout the world are basically alike. Everyone wants to be loved, appreciated, and respected, and I am a better person because of the years I spent in the air. God blessed me with a career I loved, and I was able to enjoy it for thirty-four years.

Lastly but most importantly, I am thankful to God for keeping me safe on those many flights. He is the one who is ultimately in control of our fate!

Afterword

As I finish this book, life is on hold because of the Covid-19 pandemic. It has extensively affected air travel, especially international flights. The airline industry and the whole world are mastering social distancing. Life is so different. We will hopefully see restrictions end soon so our lives and the economy can return to normal. While the pandemic has brought horrific sadness, death, and illness to the entire world, many have managed to find some positive aspects amidst the dire circumstances. People have shared with me that they have spent more time with their families, undertaken new exercise regimens, and completed long-overdue projects. One of my small positives is that I was able to finish my book, which has taken me over two years to do.

In the course of my writing, I lost my younger brother, Gary. He died a few months ago, and I can still hear him asking me about my trips. "Sis, you have any funny stories to tell me?" I would share my anecdotes, and he would always tell me I should write a book.

Well, sweet baby brother, I have written and finished this book, and I dedicate the funny stories to you. We will forever feel a void not having you with us, but I look forward to seeing you again one day in our forever home in Heaven.

Losing a loved one is unbelievably hard, but it is easier to process when you know you will see them again. That is the promise of God in His Word. "If I go and prepare a place for you, I will come back and take you to be with me that you also may be where I am." ~ John 14:3 NIV. Praise God for His mercies, protection, and His promise of eternal life!

Brief Airline Histories

PIEDMONT AIRLINES TIMELINE

Piedmont has an interesting history. It was founded by Thomas Henry Davis (1918-1999) in Winston-Salem, North Carolina. In 1940, he purchased Camel City Flying Service and changed the named to Piedmont Aviation, where he worked as a flight instructor. Camel City had originally operated as an airplane repair service and training school for pilots in the War Department Civilian Pilot Training Program.

Until the late 1970s, airlines were not regulated, and the "hub" system in place now did not exist. The early routes at Piedmont stretched northwest from Wilmington, North Carolina, to Lynchburg, Virginia. Piedmont's first jets took off in March of 1967, and from then on, their Boeing 727-100s were used on routes to Atlanta, Asheville, Winston-Salem, Roanoke, and New York.

Piedmont purchased one notable Boeing 727-100 from Northwest Orient Airlines. It was the very jet hijacked by D.B. Cooper, who exited via parachute through the back hatch with his stash of stolen money. I flew on that aircraft in 1986 and enjoyed hearing the story of Cooper's escape from the other members of the crew.

Other key dates in Piedmont's history were:

- 1944: Davis filed for an application to run a passenger flight service.

- 1948: The first flight from Wilmington, North Carolina to Cincinnati, Ohio. All flights were on the Douglas DC-3 aircrafts until 1958.

- 1967: Purchased first Boeing 727-100s.

- 1968: Purchased first Boeing 737-200s.

- 1982: After the last YS11 flight, they became all jet service. After deregulation in the late 1970s, the airline grew rapidly and developed a hub at Charlotte/Douglas International Airport in Charlotte, North Carolina.

- 1984: Piedmont started flying to the west coast on the 727-200s with first class service.

- 1985: Piedmont bought Empire Airlines, which brought Fokker F-28s into the fleet.

- 1987: Began Charlotte to London Gatwick Airport service. Several commuter and regional airlines provided passenger feed for Piedmont via code sharing agreements.

- 1989: Piedmont was absorbed by USAir (formerly

Allegheny Airlines). USAir would later change their name to US Airways.

US AIRWAYS TIMELINE

US Airways traces its history to All American Aviation, Inc., a company founded in 1939 by the du Pont family brothers, Richard C. du Pont and Alexis Felix du Pont Jr. All American Aviation was headquartered in Pittsburgh and served the Ohio River Valley.

Other key dates in US Airways' history were:

- 1949: All American Aviation changed its name to All American Airways and switched from airmail to passenger service.
- January 1, 1953: All American Airways changed its name to Allegheny Airlines
- 1972: Allegheny Airlines absorbed Mohawk Airlines, making it one of the largest carriers in the northeastern United States. By 1973, it was the ninth largest airline in the free world.
- 1979: Allegheny Airlines changed its name to USAir and became the world's largest operator of the DC-9 aircraft.
- 1984: USAir took delivery of the first Boeing plane.
- 1986: USAir purchased Pacific Southwest Airline (PSA). This acquisition was completed on April 9, 1988.
- 1987: USAir purchased Piedmont Aviation, Inc.
- 1988: In September 1988, USAir flew to ninety-five

airports from hubs in the eastern United States.

- 1989: On August 5, 1989, Piedmont Airlines was fully absorbed by US Air, formerly known as Allegheny Airlines.

- 1990: USAir consolidated its headquarters, moving from Washington National Airport to a new building nearby in Crystal City in Arlington County, Virginia. Maintenance and operations headquarters remained at Pittsburgh International Airport.

- 1995: USAir returned to profitability and continued to expand its flights to Europe until the end of the decade.

- 1997: USAir changed the name of US Airways, and a new corporate identity was launched. The aircraft were all painted a deep blue and medium gray with red and white accent lines. The airline further expanded when America West Airlines carried out a reverse merger in 2005 and acquired the assets and branding. The America West leadership team were largely in charge of the merged airline of US Airways. US Airways also bought the remains of the Trump Shuttle.

- 2001: After the September 11 terrorist attacks and the closure of one of their largest hubs in Washington, D.C., thousands of employees were furloughed.

- 2002: US Airways entered Chapter 11 bankruptcy on August 11, 2002. After receiving a government-guaranteed loan through the Air Transportation Stabilization Board, the airline exited bankruptcy in 2003.

- 2004–2005: US Airways once again filed for bankruptcy and merged with American West Airlines. The merger was complete in 2007.

- 2015: With growth and a route expansion that continued throughout the years, US Airways and American merged.

AMERICAN AIRLINES TIMELINE

American Airlines got its beginning in 1930 with a union of more than eighty small airlines. The two organizations from which American Airlines originated were Robertson Aircraft Corporation and Colonial Air Transport. These companies merged in 1929, forming The Aviation Corporation, which was turned into an operating company and rebranded as American Airlines. Between 1970 and 2000, it grew to be an international carrier that purchased Trans World Airlines (TWA) in 2001.

C.R. Smith, the CEO of American Airlines, played an instrumental part in developing the DC-3. He made a call to Donald Douglas and persuaded him to design a sleeker aircraft based on the DC-2, a design intended to replace American's Curtiss Condon II biplanes. In return, American agreed to purchase twenty of these new aircraft.

American again made history when it introduced the DST on December 17, 1935, the 32nd anniversary of the Wright Brothers' flight at Kitty Hawk. That airplane eventually became the DC-3, a plane that changed the industry because American was able to switch their main revenue stream from mail to passenger service on June 26, 1936.

In 1945, American operated service for the first time with American Overseas Airlines, and in 1957, it opened the world's first special facility for flight attendant training.

The facility was called the American Airlines Stewardess College, located in the Dallas–Fort Worth area of Texas.

Other key dates in the history of American Airlines were:

- January 1970: American merged with Trans Caribbean Airways and gained routes to the Caribbean.
- November 1, 1984: American introduced the American Eagle system, a commuter system that serviced smaller and short-range destinations.
- December 20, 1989: American announced plans to expand its Latin American service with routes from Eastern Airlines.
- March 27, 1991: The airline recognized its billionth customer.
- September 11, 2001: American Airlines tragically lost 23 people, including pilots, flight attendants, and family members during the terrorist attack that involved Flights 11 and 77. This one day changed the world of aviation history.
- 2011: AMR Corporation, the parent company of American Airlines, filed for bankruptcy protection.
- 2013: American Airlines merged with US Airways but kept the American Airlines name because the management of both companies considered American to be the better-recognized name brand in both the domestic and international markets. The combined assets of the two airlines resulted in the creation of the largest airline in the world.
- October 16, 2015: US Airways Flight 1939 flew as the last service of an independent airline. On the same day, American and US Airways began operating as one

airline with a Single Passenger Service System.

- January 17, 2017: Air Transport World named American Airlines the 2017 Airline of the Year.
- September 4, 2019: American retired the last of its MD-80 aircraft after thirty-six years as the workhorse of the airline's fleet.

Works Cited

California Integrated Seismic Network (CISN). June 15, 2004. "2004 M5.3 Earthquake South of Coronado, CA" https://www.cisn.org/special/evt.04.06.15/

Elliott, Frank. Compiled by Norfleet, Elizabeth K. *Piedmont: Flight of the Pacemaker*. Published February 20, 2006 by Piedmont Aviation Historical Society.

Harlan, Chico. "Landing a mega merger: The last days of US Airways." The *Washington Post*. September 25, 2015.

Ibay, Allec Joshua. YouTube. May 12, 2017. "The Los Angeles Runway Disaster" https://www.youtube.com/watch?v=8FCHQL2aezc

Logan, Gabi. "Travel Tips: The Effects of 9-11 on the Airline Industry." *USA Today*. https://traveltips.usatoday.com/effects-911-airline-industry-63890.html Updated April 24, 2018.

National Weather Service. April 26, 1991. "Top Ten KS Tornadoes" https://www.weather.gov/ict/toptenkstors

The Piedmont Aviation Historical Society. Accessed 2020. https://www.digitalnc.org/institutions/piedmont-aviation-historical-society/

Richter, Paul. The *Los Angeles Times*. "LAX Crash prompts FAA Safety Rules for Runways." February 16, 1991.

Wikipedia. Accessed 2020. "US Airways History." https://en.wikipedia.org/wiki/US_Airways

Wikipedia. Accessed 2020. "History of American Airlines." https://en.wikipedia.org/wiki/American_Airlines

Wikipedia. Accessed 2020. "Evacuation of US Airways Flight 1549." https://en.wikipedia.org/wiki/US_Airways_Flight_1549

Wikipedia. Accessed 2020. "1989 Loma Prieta earthquake." https://en.wikipedia.org/wiki/1989_Loma_Prieta_earthquake

Acknowledgments

Special thanks to Catherine Gauldin and Anne McAneny, my editing and formatting team, who helped prepare my book for publishing. I will always be thankful for your help and the many hours you spent to make this book possible.

Many thanks too to Rick Kersten, artist, illustrator, and cartoonist. I fell in love with his art when I started flying in 1984 and purchased *The Stewardess*, which serves as the front cover of my book.

About the Author

Sharon Carroll Williams was a flight attendant for a major airline for more than thirty-four years, from 1984–2018. She lives in Virginia with her husband, Dale. Together they have four children and eight grandchildren.

Special request from Sharon: If you enjoyed this book and would like to post a review on the site of your choice, I would very much appreciate your time and effort. Reviews are difficult to come by but they're invaluable in connecting books with readers. Thank you! *~Sharon*

Made in the USA
Coppell, TX
30 September 2021